My Nana's Voice

An Irish girls' journey from Maiden to Mother to Crone

A Memoir.

My Nana's Voice

An Irish girls' Journey from Maiden to Mother to Crone

A Memoir.

by
Alicia McMahon

Acknowledgements

First and foremost, I would like to thank Séanalee and Brennalynn for allowing me to share our story. I love ye both so much and thanks for being such awesome daughters. Both of you are my ultimate gift in life.

Nana Murphy You diamond you. – I keep hearing your words of wisdom and your voice guiding me every day. I know you are with me and that comforts me. Thank you. I love you.

I also wish to thank my Mammy, Daddy and my four sisters' Tina, Jenny, Kim and Amy for keeping me going when times got hard. Without your love and support morally and emotionally through the years, I would not be the woman I am today. Family is all we have and without ye I would be lost. Thank you for being there for me through thick and thin. I love ye all so much.

I would like to thank all those whose assisted me along the way over the past 6 years of writing. Especially my best friend in the whole wide world Debbie Follenweider. Debbie is my biggest supporter and has been by my side for the last twenty plus years. My #6 sister, I love you.

And finally, I want to give a special thanks to the love of my life Dennis Hohman. Although, I think he would prefer if I labeled him as my last chance of happiness. Denny without you, I would still be dilly dallying and finding excuses why not to publish. Weekend after weekend reading and editing for years. It was your endless support and holding me accountable is what made this happen. Thanks for believing in me Denny.

Introduction

In the end, in the beginning, it is all about guidance. And hope.

On the cover of this book sits a spiraling Celtic symbol, the *Triskle*. This symbol is speculated to be the oldest symbol of spirituality, even before the *Trinity*. The *Triskle* evokes the Druidic Threefold Mother Goddess, representing the stages in a woman's life, which all derive from one:

The Maiden, The Mother and The Crone.

My *Crone Voice* has miraculously guided me throughout my life's journey. On that journey, over two continents, I have found myself in scary and life-wrenching situations over which I had no control. And in turn, having had to make numerous life-changing decisions based upon these situations, this center is where I try to find insight.

I have something deep inside me driving me to write my story. I'm not sure why, but I have learned through the years that I have to listen to that inner voice. Some people call it intuition. Some call it a gut feeling. I call it my *Crone Voice*.

I consider myself a normal person with what I feel are good morals and values, just trying to make it through this journey we call life. I truly try to live righteously and be a better person every day. I am a mother of two astounding young women, Seanalee and Brennalynn. They, too, have served as my guides, time and again. As such, this is *our* Journey.

A wise man once said:

"Writing a memoir is like preparing yourself to go to confession." ~ Frank McCourt

So here I go.

In the name of the Father, the Son and the Holy Spirit. It has been twenty-two years since my last confession...

TABLE OF CONTENTS

TABLE OF CONTENTS (continued)

Chapter 1

The Legend - Nana Murphy

*"It's time for **you** now, luv. You can't give up on taking*

care of you and your happiness just because you are a

Mammy. I think it's time to cut the apron strings."

The year was 2010. I woke up one Saturday morning in my

townhouse in Lafayette, Colorado, opened my curtains and then

looked into my youngest daughter Brennalynn's bedroom to find

her still sound asleep. My eldest daughter Séanalee had just moved

out of the house and a few weeks earlier. I quietly closed the door

1

and walked down the stairs to put on the coffee. I got to the end of the stairs and had just turned right to open the blinds in the sitting room when I spotted a yellow sticky note on the sitting room table. I picked up the note. It read:

"Nana's Tribute, Lysh do it. Call T.T. today!"

I could not believe it. This was in my handwriting! When did I write this?

I remembered going to bed last night. I wasn't on the sauce and I don't do drugs…what the heck is going on? I sat on the couch and read the sticky note about five more times. I was so perplexed on how this came about. How the hell did this get there?

My beautiful Nana Murphy was born Jenny Jensen in Kolding, Denmark on October 5th, 1922. She moved to Ireland in her early twenties and met her husband, Patrick Joseph Murphy. They had eight children--Seamus, Marie, Tony, Collette, Miriam, Finbar, Desmond and Patrick before my Grandad passed away. He passed unexpectedly in his 40's, so Nana stepped right into the role

2

of Matriarch of the Murphy's and raised her large clan. She was a very well-respected woman in our little community. As a matter of fact, she was the very first woman in Ireland to hold a taxi license as well as one of the first women to be an officer and accomplished diver in the Limerick Branch of the Red Cross. What a legend! Everyone who knew my Nana called her a *Lady*.

I was pretty sure the note had to do with the dream I'd had a couple of nights before.

In my dream, I saw myself reading a tribute to my beautiful Nana Murphy in Foynes church. I saw her in the coffin before me, her lifeless expression, her peaceful beautiful body just lying there. I was standing at the podium on the altar, telling her what she meant to me. I was speaking about how much she'd influenced me throughout my entire life. I just could not stop crying through my words. My dream was so vivid I could even smell the frankincense and myrrh in the church. I gazed at her lifeless body and said, "I wish you were with me now, Nana, so I could tell you what you meant to me in person."

I woke up that next morning and was very upset by my

dream. All that day, I couldn't stop thinking about it. Now, I realize what I was telling me to do. I needed to tell my Nana how much I love her *now*. So, I decided I was going to put together a Tribute Book for my Nana Murphy, and I wanted every one of her family to participate if they desired to. I really didn't know at the moment why I needed to do this, but I just knew I had to.

Later that afternoon, I sent a text to my sister Tina in Ireland and asked her to call me when she had a chance. She called me later that day and I explained everything to her. She was completely on board and was going to help me contact all the family. Lord, I didn't know what I was getting into. The majority of The Murphy family still lived in my hometown, a village in Foynes, County Limerick, Ireland. I had four first cousins living in different countries and then I lived in the U.S.

I eventually collected everyone's submissions and put them all into a book. I was just going to produce one book and one book only. This was so my Nana would have the only copy in the world. The book came together rather nicely. We had 86 family members submit something. I received poems, essays, one liners and pictures. I put them all together chronologically for Nan's one-of-a-kind book. It started with Uncle Seamus, her eldest son, and it ended with a picture of my niece Jody's ultrasound which said, "I can't wait to meet you, Nana Murphy. Love, Jodie Wilmott."

It's such a beautiful homage for a beautiful lady.

Over the years, Nana was everyone's center, everyone's guide, as well as being everyone's disciplinary figure. On the weekends, we all would eventually make our way to Nana's house, especially on Sundays. I remember this one particular Sunday. It was very windy and cold. I made my way over to Nana's house for a cup of tea and a warm fire.

I walked in the back door. Uncle Dessy and Uncle Patrick were playing a game of scrabble in the chairs surrounding the fire. Nana was sitting on the couch crocheting. It looked like my uncles were about mid-game. There were two dictionaries at the ready just in case they needed to prove a word was correct--both the big

Oxford dictionary and the popular Webster dictionary.

Sometimes their debate became so heated you could hear the racket from outside the house. It was mostly my uncles disagreeing with themselves, but when Nana raised her voice, as she did occasionally, everyone listened. I watched the game intensely. I must have been around ten or eleven years old at the time, and because I was quiet and sitting with my back up against the wall in the nook of the kitchen, I think they all forgot I was there. They were really getting into it.

My Uncles Patrick and Dessy were both barrel-chested men, both about 5'1" to 5'3" tall, in their mid-thirties. Both had hearty, contagious laughs and were comfortably boisterous.

"That's not a fucken word Patrick, get out of it, will you!" Dessy exclaimed.

"It's a word Des. I'm telling you 'tis," Patrick insisted.

"Mammy is that a word?" Dessy asked.

Nana said, "I don't think it is, luv."

Uncle Patrick turned directly around to the kitchen and said, "It is, Mam. I'll bet if we called Tony over, he'd tell us it is."

"Ah, bringin' the older brother in to this won't save you, Patrick," Uncle Dessy said with a grin on his face as he pointed his finger directly at his brother.

"He'll fucken set this straight, so he will," Uncle Patrick said as he raised both his hands in the air.

"Stop it, both of ye! So what does the dictionary say then...?" Nana asked, or should I say, instructed.

Uncle Dessy swiftly grabbed the dictionary and looked it up. I saw him glance over at Uncle Patrick, look back at the dictionary and then up at Nana before sheepishly admitting, "Oh wait...it says it's a word."

"Go away, you bollocks! Dessy, you should have looked there first before arguing with me," bragged Patrick.

"You are talking out your cake hole, Patrick."

"I'm talking out my cake hole? I'm the one who's in the right here," my Uncle Patrick said half laughing, trying to get a rise out of Uncle Dessy.

All of a sudden Nana slammed her hand on the table. I jumped out of my skin--it was that loud. She raised her voice and said, "Enough! Both of ye. Enough! Ye are giving me no peace, for feck sake."

'Twas fierce funny for me to see both my uncles put their heads down and say, "Sorry Mam," in unison, while at the same time glaring at each other accusingly across the table.

That day I saw the raw power that my Nana had over everyone. Within two minutes, the scene went back to normal and eventually everyone was called home for Sunday afternoon dinner.

Nana's house was barely 600 square feet. It was a very quaint home with two small bedrooms one bathroom and a kitchen/sitting area. From the outside, it was one door surrounded by two windows. She had a lot of plants on the windows and she had those little troll dolls spread throughout the house. There were lots of pictures of her children, grandchildren and great grandchildren everywhere. There was barely a space in the house that didn't have a picture, plant or decoration covering it.

Nana was mostly warm, welcoming and soft, but when she got angry or heated about something her Danish accent appeared instantly.

That being said, she was humble and wise, too. I always had Nana to go to if I had a hard decision to make.

Once the tribute book was complete, I sent it in the post to Nana's house and let my first cousin, Toni Murphy, or "Mutt" as I call her, know it was on the way. Mutt lived across the road from Nan. She took care of her every day as Nana was starting to need a little help. When the book arrived, Mutt told me that Nan took it into her bedroom and kept it there. All I wanted was for her to have it close. I wanted her to know what she meant to all of us. I wanted her to feel loved, unique and special.

I was able to go home to visit everyone a few months later. I couldn't wait to talk with my Nana and see if she liked her tribute book. I was visiting Mutt and planned on staying at her house, so we could have wine and chat about the good ol' days, as we tended to do when I went home.

It was about half-past seven and I told Mutt I was going across the road to have a drink with Nan. I filled my glass of wine at Mutt's house and headed over for my long-awaited visit. I couldn't wait to see her, I was so happy.

I walked in the door and that familiar Nana's house smell hit me. It reminded me of celery, that same smell I remember from my Great Grandmother's (Nana's Mammy) house in Limerick City back in the day. I closed the front door and yelled, "Hello, is there a Nana who belongs to me in here?"

I opened the sitting room door, looked to my right and there was the beautiful lady sitting by the fire in her armchair with rosy cheeks and a smile that would melt butter.

"Well, Nana, how the bleeden hell are ya?" I said with such excitement in my voice.

I will never forget the excited expression I got in return. I went over and hugged the crap out of her and gave her a big ol' kiss on her soft old-lady cheek. I was so, so happy to see her. I felt

blessed to be with her. I put some turf on the fire and said,

"Well, Nan, do you want an ol' tasheen as we sit and chat by the

fire?"

"You know what, luv…I would love a drop of Hennessey.

There is some in the press under the telly," she replied softly, with

a smile on her face.

"Ahh… Brilliant, Nan. You're a diamond, you never lost

it!"

I poured her brandy in her favorite brandy glass and handed

it to her. I sat in the other armchair by the fire with my glass of

wine. We had the most beautiful time. We were so happy to be

together. There was an understanding with each other that didn't

always need words. Silence was not uncomfortable between us.

Although, I'm not going to lie, I kept waiting for her to

bring up her book, but she didn't, so I didn't ask.

She was such a lady. She announced that her hair was a

mess. I replied to her with, "Jesus, Nan, don't you think you could

have at least put on a bit of lipstick and got the hair curled when you knew I was coming over to see you?" I joked with her like that all the time and she loved it.

She replied with, "Go 'way, you little strap!"

We laughed and laughed that night and had such a great time. After about a couple of hours, the atmosphere became a little somber. We both sat contently, gazing into the fire and sipping our tasheens. I think she was just getting tired, as it was late in the evening for her. I could hear her clock ticking and the fire crackling as I gazed into the warm hearth.

Then Nan looked over at me, smiled and asked, "Alicia luv, are you ever going to come home to Ireland? Séanalee is nineteen and Dowser is seventeen now. Isn't that when you started your journey?"

"I don't know if I will, Nan. I don't know what my plan is yet," I replied sincerely.

"Do you have a man in your life now, Darlin'?"

"No. No I don't, Nana. I just don't want to introduce the girls to anyone else until they get sorted with school."

"You're a good girl, Alicia. You have always had a good head on your shoulders." She paused, looked at the fire and then over at me and asked, "Can I give you some advice Darlin'?"

"Of course, you can, Nan."

"It's time for *you* now, luv. You can't give up on taking care of *you* and your happiness just because you are a Mammy. I think it's time to cut the apron strings."

"Okay, Nan," I said, even though I did not know what she was referring to. I was very confused about what she meant, but I acted like I understood what she was saying. She looked at me with those piercing light-blue eyes and then she slightly nodded her head and smiled at me like I understood what she was telling me.

About ten minutes later, I put some coal on the fire to keep the house warm while she was in bed. I put the grate in front of the fire and went into her bedroom to get her night robe. I walked into her room and turned towards her bed.

There was the book on her nightstand. I felt a pulse in my

heart. I think it skipped a beat. I put my hand on it and gently caressed the picture of her face on the front cover. I wanted to pick it up and bring it out to her, so we could read through it together, but I didn't. Something stopped me. I knew if she wanted to do that she would have brought it up to me already.

I grabbed her pink silky robe, the one with the embroidered flowers on it, off the back of her bedroom door and returned to the sitting room.

"Here's your robe, Nana," I said, as if I didn't see the tribute book on her nightstand. I helped her put it on, tied the belt in a loose knot, made her a cup of tea and set it by her chair. By this time, my wine glass was well empty, and I felt like I was spittin' feathers. I was parched.

"Nana, will you be all right if I leave? Do you need anything before I go back over to Mutt's House?"

"Sure, I'm grand now. I will head into bed here soon after I drink my tea, luv."

"Right so Nan, I'll head out." I walked over to her, hugged

her tight for about thirty seconds, kissed her and whispered, "I love you so much, Nana."

I felt the tears flood my eyes and instantly felt that lump in my throat, the lump that does not give you a choice…you know, that feeling, right?

I think Nana felt my emotion. She turned her head slightly towards my ear. "I love you too, darling. Follow your dreams, Alicia, and heed my words," she whispered.

As I walked to the door, I turned around to get another look at her and snapped that picture in my head. I am smiling as I write this because I still see her by the fire in her pink robe with a beautiful warm smile on her face.

I walked back across the road to Mutt's and poured another hearty glass of wine.

"Well Lysh, how'd it go? How is she doing? Did she bring up her tribute book?" Mutt asked me as I was walking into the kitchen.

I was trying to ignore that huge lump in my throat and act normal. "She didn't mention anything Mutt, not a word about it."

"Well she told me it was one of the kindest things anyone has ever given her and she wants it to be buried with her," Mutt said.

I looked right at her and said, "Are you serious, Mutt? That is just beautiful!"

She must have loved it. I hoped she would have. I wondered again why she didn't say anything about it to me.

"If you listen hard enough, the heart will speak to you."

~ Alicia McMahon

Chapter 2

Growing Up in Foynes and Shanagolden

"The color of the Irish pound was just lovely, 'twas even more lovely because 'twas all mine."

On the same day Charlie Chan passed away and Carly Simon's song *You're so Vain* was #1 on the charts, the world was blessed with the birth of Alicia Miriam McMahon, in other words….ME! I was born at the maternity hospital in Limerick City, Ireland. At that time, I was the youngest of three girls, and was, in fact, my Daddy's favourite, which is as true today as it was

then. Tina is my eldest sister, then Jenny, pronounced Yenny (if

you read through the book calling her Jenny, she will probably go

mental,) and then me, Alicia (Lysha.) I was the youngest for about

twelve years and then Mammy and Daddy had Kim and then Amy.

Mam also had a little boy in-between Tina and Jenny who passed

away soon after she gave birth. She named him Patrick Joseph

after her Father, Patrick Joseph Murphy. Mam and Dad still speak

of Patrick Joseph today, just as my sisters and I do.

I grew up in a quaint little Irish Parish in County Limerick,

with rolling hills, little cottages, a stone church and one main

street. There are three townships in St. Senan's Parish. One village

is called Foynes and is located on the bank of the majestic River

Shannon. It was one of the biggest import/export locations in

Ireland at one time. The second village is Shanagolden, which is

three miles inland from Foynes. The third is Robertstown, which is

about two miles from the other villages. During my childhood I lived in both Foynes and Shanagolden.

My Daddy's name is Hugh McMahon. Daddy is about 5'10", slender (at one time) in stature, has soft eyes, good hair and a genuine smile. On a quick judgment...he's a warm person overall. He grew up in a town called Abbeyfeale in County Limerick. Daddy's family owned a butcher shop on the main street on the way into Abbyfeale town and it is still there to this day. Daddy's family also transported stuff in trucks. I don't know exactly what they transported, but Daddy has some stories about smuggling cattle in and out of Northern Ireland. We were never allowed to talk about that stuff. Oops.

My Mammy's name is Miriam Murphy McMahon. Mammy was born and raised in Limerick City and then moved to the village of Foynes where her daddy bought the local hotel and bar called The Shannon House. It stands on the main street in Foynes right next to the harbor. It's still there and is thriving to this day.

We lived a very modest life. From the age of fifteen, Daddy was a truck driver working for his father. Then he went on to drive for Mervin Black and then Molloy & Sherry trucking companies. They hauled meat from the harbor up the country and sometimes overseas. He would drive to other continents for weeks at a time, leaving my Mam to care for us on her own. Sometimes we would have bread and sugar with a cup of tea for dinner. I loved it and I didn't see anything wrong with it. I will still throw some sugar on bread and butter once in a while as an adult. There were a few times when Mammy would ask us to go over to Nana's house and ask her for some bread and Jam. Oftentimes she would not see Daddy's wages until he got back from his trips abroad. That said, we would have an abundance of food when Daddy did come home with his paycheck in hand. We would have meat, potatoes, cabbage, milk and sometimes even cereal for breakfast. Mammy would only buy Corn Flakes or Rice Krispies. She would never buy the cereal with chocolate or marshmallows in it. Not that we would ever complain about Corn Flakes--we all loved them.

At times, Daddy would barter with the foreign sailors who docked their boats in Foynes Harbor and bring home boxes of goods. One time, he brought home a big box of bananas and Jenny and I went to town on them. We would eat green bananas for days. He also used to bring home peppermint-flavored Orbitz gum. To us that was kiddo Caviar.

Growing up, there were some rough times, moneywise. Mam would even hide from the rent man. He would come once a week for the rent money. 'Twas primarily on Fridays. When Mammy didn't have any money, she would warn us not to open the door. On more than one occasion, she would point her finger, pucker her lips and say with such conviction, "Don't let him know we are home! I'll have yer guts for garters!"

We didn't have a car or even a telephone, so it was hard for someone to know if anyone was home to collect the money owed. We didn't have heating in the bedrooms, either, but there was a fireplace in the kitchen and one in the sitting room. If we wanted to get warm or dry we would literally have to stand in front of the fire for warmth.

When we got a little older, Daddy took a job driving for Estuary Fuel. It was a local company based in Foynes, but he still travelled nationally across all of Ireland.

Considering you can drive from the northernmost tip of Ireland to its southern peninsula in less than twelve hours, it worked better for raising a family. And I'll bet my Mammy was tired of the long weeks alone trying to raise us by herself, as well as listening to Daddy's stories and adventures when he got back. I know it was hard on her.

There was one night--I can't actually remember how old I was, but I must have been around five or six at the time--when I woke up out of the blue and went downstairs to the sitting room. There were three rooms downstairs in our house--sitting room, kitchen and bathroom. And there were three very small bedrooms upstairs. Yeah, it was a small house. We always had to close the doors to each room to try and contain what heat we had from the two fires downstairs. On this particular evening, I opened the sitting room door, and there was Mammy, sitting on the armchair by the fire. She was obviously crying about something as I saw her wipe her eyes as soon as I opened the door.

"What's wrong, Mam?" I asked in my sleepy voice.

"Nothing, Alicia. Everything is fine. Go on now and up the stairs with you," she ordered in a stern voice. It wasn't the *real* stern voice. 'Twas the kind of stern voice that wasn't mad at me, but stern all the same.

"Are you okay, Mam? Are you crying? Is everything all right?"

"'Tis, luv. I'm just waiting up for your Daddy. He should be home soon. Come on in and warm up by the fire for a minute."

I couldn't believe it. She actually asked me to come in and sit with her. This never happened. I felt so special at that moment. I sat with Mam, and she asked me about school and how things were with my friends, and she even asked me about my best friend Mutty, who was also my cousin. I think this was one of the first grown-up conversations I had with Mammy and I loved it! I stayed in the sitting room with her for about thirty minutes just chatting away together. Then we both heard someone at the front door.

Lo and behold, 'twas my Daddy! He was home from work!

I rushed over and jumped right into his arms. He had his work pants, boots and jacket on. He smelled like oil and smoke from cigarettes, or as we call cigarettes in Ireland, fags.

"Daddy, you're home! Did you get me anything? Did you bring me a present?" I asked with sheer excitement.

"I will show you tomorrow, luv. What are you doing up so late, anyway?" he asked.

"I couldn't sleep, Daddy, and Mammy said I could sit by the fire for a while to warm up."

Then I looked over at Mammy and she was staring at the fire. I knew something was wrong, I just didn't know what it was. Mammy looked straight at me and said,

"G'wan, Lysh. Off up to bed with you."

Disappointed, I looked down at the carpet with a cute, sleepy expression on my face and said, "Okay, Mam." I kissed Mammy and kissed and hugged Daddy and I went back up to bed. I tried to listen to what they were saying from my bedroom by putting my ear to the floor, as my room was directly above the

sitting room, but the voices were too muffled. I fell asleep right
there on the floor.

I was so excited about the experience I'd had with Mammy that
night and Tina and Jenny didn't. Ya know when you have a
moment with a loved one that you hold dear to your heart growing
up? Well that was my one.

As my sisters and I got a little older, Mam and Dad were
able to afford a car. I think, if I remember correctly, it was a
Volvo. So that meant we were not as desperate anymore. Daddy
was home every night, which meant a real dinner, not a bread and
sugar dinner, since Daddy would never stand for that on his table.
And there would always be a fire on when it was cold. We would
have baths on Saturdays and then Mass on Sundays. Things were
predictable and regular now. Sunday dinner was always roast
chicken, both mashed and roasted spuds, vegetables, gravy and
stuffing. We would even have dessert. Daddy loved prunes with
cream or rhubarb tart. He always liked his desserts. To this day, he

still likes a sweet after dinner.

Mammy would always brush our hair and dress us similar to each other. She took pride in her girls and always made sure we were well-dressed and well-spoken. She would spend so much time having us pronounce things correctly without the country accent. THis, THat, THese and THose, NOT dis, dat, deezs and dose. It would drive her MAD if she heard us pronounce those words incorrectly or with the culchie country farmer accent.

Bless her heart. Mammy was very adamant that Tina, Jenny and I save money--not that we had a lot of it, but she wanted us to strive to know the value of saving.

I will never forget the first time Mammy took me down to the Bank of Ireland on the main street of Foynes to open my very first bank account. It was right after I received my first communion. I could not believe how much money I got. I held all of it in my little hands and just looked at it in awe…all twenty-three Irish pounds. The color of the Irish pound was just lovely, and 'twas even more lovely because it was all mine.

I even got my own bankbook with my name on it. *Alicia Miriam McMahon.* It looked so official and real. God, I felt a certain sense of pride that day, even though it was all communion money and not money I earned. But this was the start of me knowing I could save my own money. Mam started giving me jobs to do and paid me for doing them. I know she did this to encourage me to save my money and earn it for myself, and do you know what? It worked.

We didn't always live in Woodvale. My family moved from Foynes Village to just outside of Shanagolden Village when I was about seven years old, for about four or five years. We bought this little cottage located at the base of the Mount of Shanid Castle. The house was derelict-looking, very small and very cold. The kitchen floor was just concrete--no linoleum or tile on it at all. Just raw cement.

It was bone chilling cold to walk on. I would run to the bathroom through the kitchen as fast as I could because it would take ages for my feet to heat back up by the fire. Jenny and I shared a bedroom that would only fit a set of bunk beds in it. There wasn't even room for a wardrobe. The door to our room was an old

barn door. It had a latch as a handle and it was high up on the door.

For about the first six months we lived there, I couldn't even reach

it! I used to keep Mammy's Encyclopedia Britannica Volume 5 by

the door, so I could stand on it and open the latch. The cottage at

Shanid was about five kilometers from Shanagolden Village.

I know this *how*, you ask? Because we had to walk to

school most of the time! It wasn't long before we all had holes in

our shoes. Sure, we put cardboard in them to cover the holes, but

we still knew they were there. Mammy and Daddy enrolled us into

Shanagolden National School. We only had one car at the time, a

little red Renault hatchback. They got rid of the Volvo. Tina, Jenny

and I would walk the back roads and pick hazelnuts and

blackberries off the bushes on the way to school. After a while

Mam and Dad got us secondhand bikes. We felt like we were high-

class folks--not having to walk and all, plus we would get to school

with dry feet, as holes in shoes were not a problem on a bike.

I have one traumatizing memory from my time living in Shanid.

Mammy and Daddy were both working, so Tina, Jenny and I were alone quite a bit in the cottage at Shanid. One day when I was seven or eight, we arrived home from school and I was starving. I had forgotten to bring my lunch that day and Jenny wouldn't share her banana sandwich with me. I was weak with the hunger, like! We didn't have a lot of food in the kitchen. There were spuds, butter, bread, milk and soy sauce in the fridge, so I decided to make some chips. Daddy used to keep the oil in the chip pan all the time. It was brown and dirty looking, but he said it added flavour to the chips. I put the chip pan on the cooker and turned on the gas. I got three big spuds and peeled them. I then cut them into chips and by the time I was done, the oil in the chip pan was so hot it was smoking. I got a handful of chopped potatoes and threw them into the smoking-hot, brown, flavoured oil and I will never forget the pain. The oil splattered all over my face. I screamed like a banshee! I could not stop screaming as I ran out the back door. I just ran in circles screaming, screaming and screaming! The pain was so bad I fell down into a fetal position and started rocking on the ground. Tina ran out to the back yard to see what had happened to me.

"Jesus Christ, Alicia, what happened?" she asked in a panicked voice.

"The chip pan oil splattered all over my face, Tina!" I said, screaming in between my sobs. She immediately ran in and took the chip pan off the cooker, then ran back out to me in the yard. She put her hand on my back and pulled my hands away from my face. I will never forget her reaction when she looked at my face. I had over 20 bubbled blisters on my face, lips eyebrows, cheeks and forehead.

My poor, beautiful face!

We didn't have a phone in our house and Tina didn't know what to do. She brought me inside and gave me a cold, wet washcloth to put on my face until Mammy came home. It seemed like hours, but finally we heard her car pull into the drive at the side of the house. Tina and Jenny immediately ran out to meet

Mam and tell her what had happened.

Mammy ran into the sitting room and rushed directly over to me, carefully removing the washcloth. "Oh Jesus, Mary and Joseph! Alicia, luv, are you okay? What were you thinking?" she asked me.

"I was starvin', Mammy. I forgot to bring my lunch to school today and Jenny wouldn't even give me a bite of her banana sandwich. I just wanted to make chips when I got home," I said, crying and sobbing and hoping for a bit of sympathy.

She looked directly at me and gently caressed my blistered face. That was the first time I'd ever seen my Mammy with tears rolling down her face. She was feeling my hurt and pain. That moment was very real to me, although she was still upset that I'd used the cooker without her being there. She said I should have known better, but she was very loving to me after that.

I still had to go to school the next day, even with my blistered face. I was so mortified that I looked like The Phantom of the Opera. My good friend Michelle Culhane stood up for me the entire day at school. She even shoved Sean Madigan after he said something mean to me about my face. I felt very vulnerable and exposed that day, but I also felt protected by my friend Michelle. She made me feel better about myself, even though I looked atrocious.

Overall things were very quiet living in Shanid. Tina, Jenny and I would explore the land and the castle grounds to overcome boredom. We would spend hours and hours out in the rolling hills playing games and making forts. It was a simple life, really.

We had no choice but to use our imaginations to entertain ourselves. Living so far from the village, we had to walk if we wanted to go anywhere. I used to walk seven miles across the country roads to meet Michelle at her family farm in Ballyneety. Michelle and I were very precocious kids and got into quite a bit of trouble whenever we got together. Her Mammy and Daddy loved me and always fed me. They were farmers, so they used to eat good meat and potatoes. There was always fresh, unpasteurized milk at the ready.

My Daddy loved Michelle as much as her Daddy loved me. He would always ask her if she would, "*ate* an egg." He would say, "Well Culhanie, how'ra getting on? Will you *ate* an egg?" every single time he saw her.

Michelle and I were kindred spirits. I learned how to drive on the Culhane's farm on a tractor. Michelle and I had to turn and pick the spuds for days on end on that farm. We would milk the cows and shovel up the cow shit, all just to earn some money to go out. Michelle's Daddy, Pat, would give us five Irish pounds as payment for working on the farm, and of course we would use the money to go to Discos. We would buy barely black tights at the shop in Creeves Cross and then back-comb our hair and saturate it with Aqua Net hair spray. That was back in the leg warmer era with Madonna being the biggest pop star ever. Michelle and I loved dressing up like Madonna. We had different color legwarmers with ankle boots and tons of bracelets and scarfs. We thought we were the shit. Her Mammy Catharine, aka Kitty, would drive us to Shanagolden Town Hall for the youth Discos. We lived to show off our Madonna look to everyone. Kitty was more like a taxi service for us at that time, whereas my Mammy would tell me, "God gave you two legs for a reason. Use them and walk, Alicia."

After about four or five years, Mammy and Daddy decided to move back down to Foynes Village to our house in Woodvale, so we could have our friends and cousins around us and not be out in the middle of nowhere. Tina, Jenny and I were just delighted. We could be around all our cousins again and live across the street from Nana. And we could play with the neighborhood kids. I looked forward to moving back to #8 in Woodvale, but I do have fond memories of the rolling fields, roadside hazelnuts and blackberries, cows and donkeys and everything else Shanid Castle had to offer.

"Honestly, it's just the simplest things in life that are needed."

~ Alicia McMahon

Chapter 3

Teenage Loves and the Lollabosher Club

We all froze in our tracks and were like statues for about a minute. Then almost at the same time we realized there was nobody there. What did we just see? What was that?

Some of my first memories are in Woodvale, Foynes. It is an estate of houses attached to each other in twos. There is a total of thirty-two houses and we lived in #8. All the Murphy's, including My Uncle Seamus and family, were in #9. My Aunty

Collette and her family were in #11. My Uncle Tony and his lot, including his daughter--my best friend Toni (Mutty)--were in #12. And Nana Murphy was in #26. We used to call it Murphyvale. There are even more Murphy's in Woodvale now in comparison to back then.

All the teenagers in our village used to go up to the national school and just hang out. The school was nestled up against the woods and it had a football field at the back. Teenagers didn't have much to do, so we would play soccer, basketball or wall tennis. More often than not, we would just hang out at the back of the school and smoke fags we'd stolen from our parents. It was always the usual suspects who had the fags. Skinner (Brian) Enright, Nora Fitz and Jenny. Toni and I were always together, inseparable for years, as a matter of fact. I christened her Mutty after we had a fit of laughing one day and she sounded like Muttley the dog. I didn't know his name was Muttley. I thought it was Mutty the dog, so that became her nickname. Mutt is three months older than I, which I remind her of to this day. If we spotted anyone up at the back of the school, she and I would grab each other so we could go up and have a puff.

At around twelve years old, I started being interested in boys. My first boyfriend was Liam "Botty" Rimmer. Well, he was the first real kiss, anyway. It happened up at the national school in the kissing corner.

One day the wind was roaring and there was a bunch of us at the back of the school where the wall would block us from the wind. One of the lads, I think it was Skinner, dared me to kiss Botty. Skinner and Botty were first cousins.

I looked at Skinner and I said, "Is it joken me, you are? I am not kissing anyone!"

"Why… are you scared to? Have you not kissed anyone before?" asked Skinner.

"Of course I have, you Numpty!" I responded immediately, trying to be all cool. "Plenty of times," I said.

"Well, so what are you waiting for, then?"

Then I looked at Botty and he didn't object--in fact, he grabbed my hand, pulled me towards him and kissed me. Then, all of a sudden, I felt his tongue in my mouth. I thought, *Oh My God, I am shifting Botty!* So, I kissed him back and felt slobber all over my chin. *Is this what kissing is like?* I wondered to myself. I think the kiss was about five seconds, but it felt like thirty seconds! I loved the fact that I was kissing.

I suppose you never do forget your first kiss, do you? Well, that relationship lasted all of about two days. I went up to school and everyone was whispering and giggling about it. I didn't mind the attention at all. I kind of liked it, actually.

That same day, Botty came up to me and asked, "Alicia, are you going to come up to the school after supper?"

"I will, I suppose," I replied with a smirk on my face. The whole rest of the school day, I was so excited. I couldn't wait to go home, do my homework, eat dinner and wash the ware, so I could go back up to the school and kiss Botty again.

I ran over to Mutt and said, "Mutty, we are going up to the

school after supper."

She looked at me and said, "I can't Lysh. I am going to Askeaton to see my Aunty Betty."

Way to have my back, Mutt!

Well, Feckit anyway, I thought to myself. *Who will come with me, then?*

I couldn't go up on my own, like. I couldn't ask Jenny, because then she would know I was a floozy and would have ammo to blackmail me later with Mammy and Daddy.

School ended, and I ran down home.

I did my spellings and maths and asked Mam what was for dinner. "Pig shit and cauliflower," she would say. Mammy always said that when we asked what was for dinner. I never knew why she would say that, but she would say it every time and then laugh at herself.

Anyway, we had breakfast for dinner that night. Daddy loved French toast with powdered sugar and lemon juice. We would have that a couple of times a month. I think it was because the eggs in the batter for the French toast along with the bread would fill an empty belly. I was delighted that I wouldn't have tons of pots and pans to clean. Mam would only use one frying pan for French toast. After dinner I washed the ware and left it on the draining board for Jenny to dry and put it away.

I went outside and looked up the road to see if I could spot anyone up at the school. It was about 6:00 pm and there was no sign of anyone. I was so excited to see Botty again and hopefully getting another shift out of him. I was very anxious. I looked up the road at the school a few more times and then finally saw some people sitting on the front wall.

Should I go up there by myself?

I wanted to kiss him again.

Why not, for feck sake? Here goes nothing!

I put on my green bomber jacket, brushed my teeth to get the burnt French toast taste out of my mouth and headed out the door. Since the school was only seven houses up I was there in less than a minute. I walked through the black gates of the school with a confidence I'd never had before. I felt grown up and mature because I had shifted a boy.

I could hear people talking at the back of the school where "kissing corner" was located. I walked over there quietly and stopped in my tracks. I could not believe what I saw! There was Skinner and Botty…and Fiona Nester. Fiona was standing in MY fecken kissing corner with her arms wrapped around Botty's neck! I couldn't fecken believe it! What a fecken bollox.

I turned right around and walked straight home and tried not to cry. I had a big lump in my throat and my eyes were watering uncontrollably. I was so mad at him for shifting her. Didn't he realize I had never, ever kissed anyone else before in my life? Why would someone do that to someone else? My very first experience kissing a boy was ruined. Just ruined.

After attending primary school in Foynes and Shanagolden, I attended secondary school in Mount Trenchard, Stella Maris' Convent of Mercy. It was also nestled in the woods just outside of Foynes on the Glin road. It was run by Nuns and it was a girls' boarding school, but unisex during the day. Sister Gabrielle was the Principal Nun and yes, I had the stereotypical experience of having my knuckles walloped with a ruler by a Nun.

I was in the locker room with Michelle Culhane changing into our PE clothes and I cursed a couple of times. I think I said the word *shit* or *feck*, and I turned around to see Sister Gabby standing there with her scowling face, just disgusted with me and my commoner language. She grabbed my ear and literally pulled me into her office across the hall, right in front of everyone. She closed her door and rapped my knuckles with an extra-large old wooden ruler. Coming from #8 Woodvale where we say *shit* and *feck* over the breakfast table, how was I supposed to know it deserved a knuckle wallop, like?

There was a strict uniform code. A blue V-neck wool jumper with the Mount Trenchard crest on it, a crisp white blouse, blue wool skirts and white knee-high socks. If you were rich, you could afford the blazer with the crest on it. You could always tell who the working families were and who the rich farmers were by who wore the blazer and who didn't.

I don't think Tina, Jenny or I had a blazer--at least, not that

I can remember, anyway.

Tina always got new clothes, including a new school uniform, and then they would get passed down to Jenny and I would always get sloppy thirds. And if you don't know what sloppy thirds all are about, try wearing clothes after my sister Jenny!

It was slim pickings to meet fellas at Mount Trenchard, unless you were looking for a farmer or a culchie. I started meeting other boys outside of Foynes. I suppose there were a couple here and there at school, but nothing to write home about.

One was Noel Darcy. Noel was the brother of my good friend Mary Darcy whom I nicknamed Molly Dodd. Their grandparents, Aggie and Jimmy, lived next door to us in #7 Woodvale. Moll and Noel lived in Limerick City, and they would come out to Foynes for the summers, Christmases and Easters to spend time with their family.

Noel and I saw each other during the summers and had a typical teenage crush and attraction. I loved being around him during the summers.

When I was around fifteen, I met Garrett Molloy. I walked into the Shannon House one day to ask Daddy for money for my badminton class at the Town Hall and there was this very tall, dark and handsome boy next to him at the bar. I immediately smiled and batted my eyes at him. My heart was pounding. He was just dreamy.

Garrett was the son of Arthur Molloy. My Daddy used to work for *Molloy & Sherry* as a truck driver in years' prior. *Molloy & Sherry* used to have all the trucks on the roads in and out of Foynes Harbor for the meat boats.

When I first met Garrett, he enamored me--initially by his height, but ultimately by his handsomeness. At age sixteen, he was 6'4" tall and extremely handsome. He was very tan with jet-black hair and beautiful brown eyes. Also, he was my Daddy's old boss's son and of course had a thick Dublin accent. I loved it. It was very different from a Limerick accent.

Garrett and I had something special. He was my first real

boyfriend. We did not have a phone in #8 back then, so I used to go to the phone box on the main street and wait for his call. I would be so excited and happy when that public phone rang. It wouldn't matter if it was pissing rain, freezing cold or gale force winds outside--I didn't care, as long as I got to talk to him.

We dated for quite a while. Garrett would come down and stay in Foynes off and on and work on the pier shunting trucks from the boats to the graveyard. *Molloy & Sherry* had a contract with The Shannon House for room and board, so he would stay there when he was in town. I loved it because he would order food and drinks and put it all on *Molloy & Sherry's* tab. We would go into the bar, play pool and order club orange and dry roasted peanuts. We would stay there for a while and then go into the restaurant and order two mixed grills almost every time we ate. A mixed grill had sausage, rashers, pork chops, beans, chips and mushrooms. 'Twas a proper heart-clogger indeed.

There was one time when Theresa Fitzsimons, who owned the Shannon House at that point in time, asked Garrett if his father knew I was eating off the company's bill.

He looked at her and replied, "You get paid, don't ya, Theresa?"

She gave him a look that would pierce stone. The cheek of her, like.

A few months later, Garrett invited me up to Dublin to attend the *Molloy & Sherry* Annual Christmas Party with him. I was so excited, I couldn't believe it, like. I was actually going up the country to Dublin! I had never been to Dublin before.

The day came, and we drove up to Dublin in one of the 18-wheeler trucks. We parked it in their truckyard a few miles from the house. Garrett's dad, Arthur, picked us up in a brand-new black Mercedes Benz. it even had a phone inside the fecken car! We didn't even have a phone in Woodvale #8! Was this really how the rest of the world lived?? I only saw things like that on the telly, like on Dallas or Dynasty!

Arthur drove us to the house and it was just beautiful. There was a windy driveway with trees on both sides and flowers and shrubs everywhere. The house was three stories high and looked like it had been designed by a famous architect.

We walked in the back door and I met Annett, Garrett's Mammy. She was so pretty and had soft, beautiful brown eyes. Her hair was perfectly-placed and she had a crisp, white-collared shirt with a beautiful blue cashmere jumper thrown over her shoulders and tied in a knot. She looked like a Hollywood movie star.

She showed me to the guest bedroom where there were built-in wardrobes with mirrors for doors and a peach sink in the bedroom in the shape of a shell. I was in awe! Who needs a sink in a bedroom? It's a far stretch from sharing bathwater with your sisters growing up like I did.

What was Garrett thinking? He had a massive house in Portmarnock, which was a very posh area in Dublin and he was dating a worker's daughter who lived in a council house with no phone. I don't actually think I had the savvy to have processed my thoughts like that back then.

Anyway, Garrett bought me a black leather women's fitted jacket as a Christmas present and I felt like a million pounds! That is, until I had to change for the Christmas Party. I had to wear one

of my Mammy's old short-sleeved going-out dresses. It was a

hideous peach color and fell just below the knee. I *borrowed* a pair

of Jenny's flat black shoes that were two sizes too big for me.

I looked a sight! I kept trying not to dance or walk too fast

or I would lose the shoes right off my feet. It was a fun night and

not a shoe lost!

The next morning, I realized I didn't want to leave there

and go back to Limerick. I wanted to stay in Dublin where there

were phones in cars and shell-shaped sinks in bedrooms.

Later that afternoon, Garrett got me a ride back to Foynes

with his friend Beni Lynch. The whole drive was about three-and-

a-half hours. Once I was back in #8, the jury had come back with

a unanimous verdict--I had wholeheartedly convinced myself that

there was more to life then Foynes, meat boats, phone boxes and

youth club discos. I felt so liberated by my experience outside of

my little village and I wanted more from life.

Garrett and I continued to have a long-distance

relationship. The only times I would get to see him was when there was a meat boat in the harbor. There was never a set schedule. Weeks, and sometimes what felt like months, would go by without a meat boat arriving in Foynes. It got harder and harder for us to keep the relationship going. The phone calls became less and less. Somewhere along the way, we lost touch completely. We ended up calling it quits and terminating our relationship.

After secondary school, Mutt and I attended the only Vocational School in Shanagolden, known as *The Teck*. I took a secretarial course, which basically taught me how to use a typewriter, how to write in shorthand (yes, I said shorthand!) and the basics of accounting.

While I was at *The Teck* I met my next love--Paul Ruttle. Paul was handsome and very funny. He had lovely brown eyes, dark skin and black hair and played soccer. There was an immediate attraction between us and we ended up dating. Paul was a popular soccer player, as was I, and we just meshed.

Mutt and I would thumb it from Foynes to Shanagolden

each morning for school. Sometimes Mutt would make us rasher butties (a bacon sandwich) in the mornings and let herself in my front door, put the kettle on and come wake me if I wasn't already up.

Isn't it funny the tasty morsels of memories that stay with you growing up? God, she was great. We would walk up to Dernish Avenue and stand by the stone wall with our thumbs out, hoping someone would give us a lift. A lot of times we would get a ride for a couple of miles up the road to Hoarns Cross, and then we would thumb it again from there to Shanagolden.

Mutt and I were like two peas in a pod. Our mothers used to ground us from seeing each other because of the sheer mischief and shenanigans we would get into. At one point, Nana Murphy got involved and told us to stay clear of each other. I could create an entire book about the tomfoolery we got up to.

Here is just one example:

One summer, the motley crew was in full swing. Out of sheer boredom, we created a little club called the Lollaboshers.

Molly Dodd, Coco, Mutt and I were all members. Coco is our other first cousin who lived in France for about fourteen years. Her Mammy is Marie Murphy, my Mammy's older sister.

Back in those days, you needed a drum of gas delivered to your house so you could hook your cooker to it. It was kind of like a propane tank for your barbeque grill. On that gas drum there was a plastic round thingamagig that we all put onto our wrists to show we were members. We also wrote a little rap about being a Lollabosher. (Remember you're a Lollabosher, remember you're a Lollabosher, remember, remember, remember you're a Lollabosher, Lollabosher!) Only those who had the wristband were allowed in our group.

This was late summer, and we would walk down to the harbor where my Uncle Tony would be. He started training to swim in the annual Shannon Estuary Swim. This was a race just over a mile that crossed the Shannon Estuary. You actually start in County Clare and end up in Foynes, County Limerick. Uncle Tony would swim in the Estuary each evening to prepare for the big swim and we, the Lollaboshers, knew this. We also knew he would have a few pounds in his wallet and we were usually hungry in the evenings.

So what I am confessing right now is that Mutt, Molly, Coco and I would head down to the harbor, wait for Uncle Tony to train in the Shannon Estuary, and then run onto the boat. Mutt would be the one who checked his wallet, since Uncle Tony was her Daddy.

After the deed was done and we were flush with poundage, back then four of five pounds went a long way. We'd walk--almost skip--with excitement over to Kelly's shop and buy a ton of sweets, fags and soft drinks. Then we would walk back to the Lady's Gate and just indulge and made ourselves sick from eating crap and smoking fags.

The Lady's Gate is about a mile outside of the village. There is a little gate in the middle of a stone wall that has a pathway that leads down to the shore. It also has a legend attached to it. It is said that people can hear a lady sobbing and crying at night and she will never rest because she lost the love of her life to the sea.

I knew starting a gang and stealing from our Uncle was not a good thing, but we were rich. A fiver or a tenner went a long way back then.

One particular summer afternoon, the Lollaboshers, minus Coco, all met up. We were ready to go get rich from Uncle Tony's wallet. I can't remember where Coco was that day, but it was just the three of us.

We were walking down the main street in Foynes just passing the church and Mutt said, "Lads, let's go to the old harbor building and check it out."

"Why would we want to do that Mutt?" I asked.

"Cuz I am fecken freezen, like!" she replied.

"Yeah, my bones hurt, it's so fecken cold," Moll said swiftly.

"Grand. So, let's go. Do you know how to get into the building, Mutt?" I asked.

"Yeah, yeah. They leave the second-floor door unlocked. My Dad brought me up here one day and told me there's not a lock on that door," she said.

So we hit up the Bank of Uncle Tony and went by Kelly's to buy some loot and then crossed over the road to the old harbor building. I remember some stories about the building being an abandoned girl's boarding school, but, that's all I knew about the building at that time. It was directly next to Foynes Hospital and across from the Railway Station.

We walked into the courtyard. Mutt led the way. We all walked up the stairs on the outside of the building. I was directly behind Mutt and Molly was behind me.

When we got to the door, Mutt pushed it open. There was a slow creak and a little bit of effort involved in opening it. She gave it a push. It opened about halfway and we all just stood there. There was very musty and stagnant smell to the building. *Creepy* is actually a better word to describe it.

Once we all got the courage to step inside, we looked left and right down a narrow hallway. At the end of each hallway there were steps up that lead to another hallway to the right and vice versa to the left. I looked at both the girls and asked,

"Are we actually doing this, lads?"

"Fuckit. We're here now, aren't we? So why not?" Moll said with conviction.

"Anything is better than that bitter fucken frigid wind," Mutty said, interrupting Moll.

We stepped into the building and closed the door behind us. It closed with that same creak, but it was easier closing than opening. Now we had to figure out which way to explore first. Left or right? We all looked to the right first, so that's the way we walked. Again, Mutt let the way.

We all turned right and walked single-file to the end of the narrow hallway, looking through each room as we passed. We got to the gable end and had to turn right and walk up the three steps to turn the corner.

This felt different. It was definitely colder and had a different sensation to it. We all paused in our footsteps and looked at each other. We were all fascinated by the building, but Mutt more so than Moll and me.

We turned the corner and started exploring the rooms. Mutt went all the way to the end and started there. I went into the first room I found and Moll went into the second room. There were two tall windows and a wardrobe in the room I went into. I looked out the window. There was just woods and trees blowing in the wind.

Mutt suddenly called out for us. "Lads, Janey Mackers, look what I found!"

Both Molly and I were in the other end of the hallway and ran over to where Mutt was. We walked into the room and there was Mutt, putting on some old-fashioned get up. She had found bags of old clothing and had started put them on. I'm serious. These clothes were from maybe the 1800's. There were a couple of long skirts sewn with proper lining and lace. They even made a swishing sound when you walked in them. There were women's blouses with frills down the front and high, tight collars. There were blazers with beautifully-covered buttons and fitted waists for women. They were all very small-sized. Molly even found a bonnet in there. That was the first time I'd ever seen stitched ribbon. The ribbon ties were silky and delicate. They had handmade stiches on them at the seams. The bonnet had a distinctly musty, moldy smell to it. I imagined who or what girl wore this beautiful bonnet. I saw Little House on the Prairie in my head.

We all got comfortable and played dress up with these amazing garments. It was so fun. We were acting the fool, pretending we were back in the good ol' days. As we were prancing around the building calling each other *Madam* and *Lady*, the mood changed almost instantly. We all felt a change in the atmosphere--the air around us was heavier and colder all at the same time. It was instant, it was obvious and it was real. We all pretty much stopped in our tracks at the same moment and looked around at each other.

Someone or something had just walked past the door.

We thought we were busted and someone had heard us in the building. I looked at Molly and put my finger up to my mouth, silently telling her to be quiet, and then I looked at Mutt and did the same. We all froze in our tracks and stood as still as statues for about a minute, though it seemed like an eternity. We could hear each other breathing and shaking.

Then almost at the same time, we realized there was nobody there.

What did we just see? What was that?

Mutt peeked out the door very slowly, looked back at us and said, "Nothing there, lads."

Molly started ripping off her skirt and blazer and said, "Feck this shit, I'm out of here!"

"Don't have to tell me twice, Moll," Mutt said.

In the meantime, I was trying to kick the skirt off and stumbled forward, making a huge thud on the wood floor.

"Fucket! Sorry lads, my bad," I said, realizing I was making a lot of noise.

Mutt instantly started her Muttley laugh and then it became a race to get out of that building.

We all ripped off the old clothes and literally ran as fast as we could out the door. I grabbed Molly and pulled her back so I could get in front of her and we both fell down on the floor. Mutt had to jump over both of us. She held out both of her hands to steady herself on each wall of the narrow hallway.

We all made it to the door and I kid you not--we couldn't open it. The fucken door was stuck! I tried to push it open, holding the latch down and shoving my shoulder into it trying to un-jam it.

Then Moll yelled, "PULL, YOU FECKEN EEJIT!"

I almost lost it, I was laughing so hard. We all rushed down the stairs and around the back of the building. The three of us were pulling each other back to get in front of the other person. It turned into a proper laugh fest after all of that. We stopped to catch our breath at the beginning of Wood Road at the back of Woodvale.

"What just happened back there?" I asked, trying to catch my breath.

"I don't want to talk about it. That shit will follow us," Molly said firmly.

"'Twill not!" Mutty said adamantly.

Whatever it was, it must have been attached to the fecken

clothes. We walked down Wood Road to Woodvale and hardly spoke a word the whole way. I know that we saw something that day, and so do Mutt and Molly. I think I felt better that we all experienced it together and it wasn't just one of us. I have not been back in that building since.

"Experience is one thing you can't get for nothing."

~ Oscar Wilde

Chapter 4

The Adventures of Mutt and Lysha

"Don't do it! I swear to God, Mutt," I whispered back at

her with my teeth clenched. Then.... She did it!

One night, Mutt and I wanted to see two boys, Paul and

John Paul. We were just bored out of our minds. There were no

friends with cars back then. As resourceful as Mutt and I were, we

decided to *borrow* a couple of bikes and peddle away on an

adventure. I took Mammy's racer and Mutt took her brother

Eddie's racer and off we went into the night.

Paul lived in Newbridge by the Thatch Bar in the middle of nowhere, and John Paul lived in Shanagolden Village. We decided to head to Newbridge first, then take the Creeves Road to Shanagolden and then circle back to Foynes from there. Foynes to Newbridge was about six or seven miles, I'd say, but when you go via Shanagolden it's a lot fecken longer.

There are no streetlights once you leave Foynes Village, so it is pitch black. We weren't able to see each other or even our hands in front of our faces. It was a weird feeling, because we both tried so hard to see our hands and we couldn't. It was a scary bike ride. The roads are so narrow, old country roads that have barely enough room for one tractor, never mind two girls on bikes who literally could not see the road they were on.

So now we were laughing and giggling over feck-all and we couldn't stop. There we were, heading into the night with two borrowed- but-forgot-to-ask-for bikes, one dodgy bike lamp and the full-on intention of seeing the two boys.

Then all of a sudden, I ripped a big fart! I literally could not control myself with laughter. It was one of those memorable farts. I was at least ten feet away from her and she still thought it was as loud as thunder. I will never forget that fart, ever! We were now in the slaphappy phase, after pulling off the bike heist and hitting the country roads.

"Mutt look at me, I'm on a fecken moped that keeps on backfiring on me. Remind me to get the spark plugs changed on it tomorrow," I said, laughing away. The tears of laughter were flowing down our cold, windburned faces.

As we hit the Creeves Road heading off the main road into the abyss, the dodgy lamp went out for good this time.

"Ahh, shit… It's banjaxed, Lysh. What do we do now?" Mutt asked.

"Either way, Mutty, we have to cycle in the dark. We can cycle and see the boys or cycle and go back to Foynes."

"Drive on, so, there's no going back," she said.

We became the two funniest comediennes alive on that road that night. Hilarious comments just flowed out of us like water from a tap.

There were a couple of close calls on the Creeves Road with some poor misfortunate farmers just trying to make their way home, turning a bend in the road and seeing a couple of girls acting the eejit on bikes.

We were about a mile outside of Creeves Cross. We knew that because there was a light in the stone quarry which was just before the cross. All of a sudden, there was a hint of moonlight, and both Mutty and I could not contain ourselves with excitement and relief that we could now see the faint blue hue that was the road in front of us.

We were ecstatic, to say the least.

"I can see you, Mutty!" I shouted.

"I can see you too, Lysh," she said.

"Check me out, Mutt, who am I? I have an alien in my basket and my name begins with an E?"

Right at that moment I started pedaling faster, waving to Mutt and acting as if I was taking off like an airplane. I was just like Elliot in the scene in the ET movie. I was laughing so hard I couldn't catch my breath.

Then all of a sudden, I was launched into the air like a missile. I hit a pothole that must have reached China. I was thrown a good five feet in front of the bike. There was complete silence and pitch black again.

I thought to myself, "Shit, I must be dead."

Then I heard, "Tell me you're all right, Lysh?"

"Oh Mutt, I'm fucked. But I'll bet it looked funny," I said.

Then we went right back into good belly-laughing and tears.

I was drenched from the water that had filled the pothole and all scratched up, and all that was on my mind was, *Mammy is going to kill me when she sees her lovely bike all banjaxed.* The front wheel was as bent as a boomerang. I picked it up and began carrying it towards Creeves Cross. We walked about a half a mile.

As we approached the bend before the cross, we saw headlights and stepped as close to the ditch as possible. The car passed, and then we heard a screech of tires and looked behind us.

The car's reverse lights came on and the car started reversing towards us. I didn't know if we should run or stay there.

The next thing I heard was, "Lysha, Toni, is that ye? What in the hell are ye doin' in the middle of nowhere in the dark?"

It was my sister Tina. At this time, Tina lived not far from Creeves Cross. She was heading down to #8 to visit Mam. We loaded up the bikes and I sat on Mutt's lap in the front of Tina's small black Fiat Panda. We got home and as per usual, faced the music. This time it was bad. Mammy was furious--not just because I'd sneaked out, but I'd also ruined her bike. Both Mutt and I were well grounded for that one. I had a two-week sentence and I think Mutt got a month! Ahh…'twas fierce funny, though. All that and we never even got to see the two boys. I wonder how long they waited?

I have another funny story about farting that I have to share from the Mutt and Lysha chronicles…

As teenagers, our Mammy's made us go to Mass every

week and report back to them on what the sermon was about, because we are good Irish Catholic girls.

It was a cold and wet Sunday morning and we were ordered to go to Mass. I walked to #12, rapped my knuckles on the door and Mutt answered.

"Are you right?" I asked.

"For feck sake its lashen rain, like," Mutt replied.

"C'mon, we're grand. Get a coat with a hood and bring the fags," I whispered so her Mammy wouldn't hear.

Off we went, walking down to the Church on the main street. We waited outside until everyone went inside and then snuck around the back of the Church and smoked our fags. We were so giddy that morning, we had to try not to laugh out loud for fear of being heard.

We waited until about halfway through Mass and then decided to sneak in at the back of the Church with just enough time to hear what the sermon was about, so we could report back to our Mammies.

"We should head in now, Lysh, or we will miss the Gospel," Mutt said, still giggling.

"Right so, in and out Mutt, no dilly-dallying," I said, trying not to laugh too loud.

We quenched our fags and popped a Wrigley's gum and headed into the Church.

We opened the outside door at the back of the Church and approached the double doors leading into the Mass.   I went to open the door on the left, but it was stuck, so I pulled harder. Then I realized it was locked and it banged loudly off the unlocked door that Mutt was opening at the same time. Everyone looked back to see what all the commotion was. We were busted!

"SHIT!" I whispered to Mutt.

We couldn't leave now, because everyone was looking at us and they all knew we were about twenty minutes late for Mass. We quietly walked a few steps up the aisle and sat down in the first empty pew. We tried to collect ourselves, which lasted a whole two minutes.

Mutt turned her head, looked at me, leaned over and whispered,

"Oh fuck. My tummy hurts, Lysh. It has been simmerin like."

I looked at her and I knew exactly what was about to happen.

"Don't do it. I swear to God, Mutt," I whispered back to her with my teeth clenched.

Then.... she did it!

It sounded like she had been holding it in for quite a while, because that fart bubbled off the flat wooden pew and the noise it made rattled the whole row. It echoed off every stained-glass pane and every beam and arch in that Church. I swear it did not sound human.

Then I realized EVERYONE had turned around and they were ALL looking right at me. There I was, sitting all alone, because Mutt had decided to lay down sideways and hide from everyone's view!

Fr. Noonan paused the sermon, looked directly at me and shook his head. I was so embarrassed and mortified. I will never forget Mrs. Clarke's face as she glared at me with sheer disgust and revulsion.

Meanwhile, that bitch lying down sideways on the pew was laughing so hard, it was like a looping clip of Muttley the dog. There I was, just sitting alone in a pew that was shaking back and forth from Mutt's uncontrollable giggling, looking back at every God-loving Catholic in my village.

I know I was viewed differently by all the parishioners after that wet and cold Sunday morning. Thanks for that, Mutt! At least the truth has finally come out! Go ahead, try and deny it!

Later that summer, I found myself in quite the predicament…

It was a lovely day in Foynes. The sun was shining, and it was so warm I decided to walk down to Kelly's Supermarket to get a 99. It was called a 99 because it cost 99 pence--it's simply a vanilla ice-cream cone with a chocolate flake stuck in the ice cream. As I was walking to the shop,

I passed Hanlon's pub and I heard an air horn from a truck. I looked behind me to see a *Molloy & Sherry* truck driving by, and there was Garrett Molloy behind the wheel, waving at me with the special trucker wave. He used to put the back of his hand up to the windshield and swing it once sternly with all five fingers separated to look like a fan.

Reactively, I waved back and just kept walking to get my delicious 99. That funny feeling in my stomach was back, just as it used to be when I was with him before. Just giddy butterflies. I got to Kelly's shop and Pauline was working behind the counter. It was either Pauline Hanley or Paddy Hughes working in Kelly's back then. I asked Pauline for a 99 and she handed it to me and asked if Noel and Mary had arrived for the summer yet. She said that Aggie, who lived in #7, was in shopping earlier and had mentioned they were coming for the summer.

Well you could have blown me over with a feather! Noel was coming for the summer again, I was going out with Paul Ruttle and Garrett had just arrived in Foynes! Jesus, Mary and

Joseph, I fecken panicked. I raced down to Mutt's house and I didn't even get to enjoy my 99. The ice cream had melted and was all over my hand from not licking it as I ran. I got to Mutt's house, ran in the front door and straight back to the kitchen.

Mutt was drying the ware. She took one look at my face and said, "What the fuck is wrong with you, girl?"

"Holy shit Mutt, I just saw Garrett and waved at him, and that was right before Pauline asked me if Noel and Moll had arrived at Aggie's yet." I was trying to catch my breath and was licking the melted ice cream off my hand at the same time.

"Well," she says, "You are really in it now, Lysh, aren't you? Sure, 'twas bound to happen, but three boys at once, good luck with that, like!"

I felt bad, because for the past three years, Noel and I had a summer romance that was very innocent, but as teenagers it was a big deal.

Mutt was still with John Paul and I was still with Paul. We all had plans to go to the disco in the youth club on Saturday night.

This happened on a Wednesday. I tried to lay low until Saturday night, but it was very hard to do in a village of five-hundred people and one of the people you were trying to avoid was next door looking out the window trying to see me.

Most of the houses in Woodvale had the net curtains so you could look out the window, but it was very hard to see inside.

Thursday evening, Mammy sent me to Kelly's Supermarket to pick up some messages. She wanted milk and butter for the morning. I fought with her as much as I could without getting a wallop, but eventually I had to give in. Mammy used her stern voice and said, "Alicia, do what you are told and go to the shop!" That, combined with her peering down over the top of her glasses, and I was on my way.

I looked out the front door, did a quick check and started walking fast. As soon as I turned the corner at Nana's house, I breathed a sigh of relief that I had not been caught by Noel. Now I needed to make it to Kelly's' without running into Garrett, because he was staying at the Shannon House, which was only a couple of doors down from Kelly's shop.

I walked into the shop and said hi to Paddy. I headed straight for the fridge area and grabbed a pint of milk and the Kerrygold butter. I turned around and saw Garrett holding a can of Fanta and a pack of Wrigley's gum.

"Well Shorty, how the bleeden hell are ya?" he said in that thick Dublin accent.

"Grand, Lofty. How's yourself?" Mammy and Daddy called him Lofty after a tall actor on the Eastenders TV show.

"Not too bad, now. How's the family?" he asked.

"Sure, they're grand, no fear of um," I replied.

"Hey, do you want to come down to the Shannon house on Saturday night for a game of pool?" he asked eagerly, for him, like.

"Yerra, I suppose I can, just get your money ready, best out of three gets a round of drinks in," I replied, trying to be cool and all that.

"Right, so see you later, then," he said with a smile.

I paid for the messages and thought to myself there was

nothing wrong with having a game of pool with my ex-boyfriend. I found myself getting excited about it as I walked home without a care in the world.

I turned the corner by Nana's and there was Noel and Molly sitting on the wall that separated #7 from #8. Trying to act normal around Noel and knowing that I had not seen Molly since last year after the dress-up Lollabosher ghost encounter at the old harbour building, I ran over to say hello. I could tell Noel was excited to see me. I said I had to go in for my supper and I asked Moll to pop over later. She came by around 6:30 for a cup of tea and I told her what was going on.

"You Bollox!" she said to me. Moll knew the story between Garrett, Paul and Noel. "You know Noel is going to the disco on Saturday at the youth club, so now what are you going to do?" she asked, half smiling.

"I haven't a clue, Moll. I do know I have to go meet Garrett for a game of pool on Saturday night at the Shannon House."

"You'll need to figure that one out, Lysh. Mutt said Paul and John Paul are going to the disco, too."

"I know Moll, I know. Maybe I'll just go to both, like," I said with my head down, not knowing exactly what I was going to do. So Saturday came and I went to play pool with Garrett. It was as if nothing had happened between us. The camaraderie was still solid, and our flirting was in full force. This made things so much harder for me.

I decided to not go to the disco and avoid two boys at once and just hang out with Garrett. We had so much fun that night. It was definitely like old times. But the next day was no fun at all. Garrett went back up to Dublin and left me to deal with my decisions, and Paul came down to Foynes looking for me. I was mortified. So (as my Mammy says, between the jigs and the reels, which in Irish-speak means, as the story goes on) I learned my lesson.

"The hardest person to be honest with is yourself.

Be yourself; everyone else is already taken."

~ Oscar Wilde

Chapter 5

Bitten by the Travel Bug

Right at that moment the room decided to spin again

and I could not help it this time.

I had to throw up, like right then and there

At fifteen, I visited my older sister Tina for a week. She was living in England. While there, I met a girl named Lisa Crawley. We hit it off and became fast friends. After I returned to Ireland, we became pen pals. She lived in a town called Kings Langley just outside of London. We wrote to each other for about a year. I loved waiting for the postman to come every day to see if I had received a letter from her. It had the queen's stamp and the airmail blue sticker on it.

I felt so important when I got a letter from Lisa. It was my special thing. I always dreamed about what she had written as she described where she lived. I would imagine myself living in a different country, away from Woodvale, a place where they had taxis and trains, a place where at night you could see many lights. It would look like Christmas every evening.

I asked my Mammy if I could go to England to see Lisa and her family. I knew Mammy felt bad about not being able to say yes. She sat down with me and explained how hard things were trying to support the family. She wished she could send all her children to a different country and give them the opportunity to experience different cultures.

As I sat in the kitchen across from her, she said, "I wish you could go, luv, but we just don't have the money for that, Alicia."

"Mammy, what if I saved my own money. Would you let me go to England then? Just for a visit over the summer?" I asked eagerly.

"Well, I suppose if you saved your own money I wouldn't stop you from going, luv," she replied without any hesitation. I knew she said that with the full understanding that I would never be able to save enough money to leave the country for the summer.

It took me less than nine months to save 380 Irish pounds. I worked two jobs, one before school and one after. Every day I had an opportunity to work, I did. I got a job at Burger Bite on the main street in Foynes. I would get up at six am and help get everything ready for the day and then I would go to school. After school, I would come home, walk up to the grotto road and make dinner for five men from Dublin. They had rented a house in Foynes since they were doing contract work on the harbour.

Those were my weekdays. Getting up early in the morning and returning home at around eight or nine at night. So many nights I would walk into #8 and feeling so tired and exhausted, but I still would have to clean the kitchen and do my homework. After a few months of seeing this, one night Mammy called me into the sitting room to talk to me.

"Alicia, luv, I know you want to save your money and go visit Lisa in England, but I think you might be pushing yourself a bit much. Your Daddy and I are just worried that you are not keeping up with school and you are not getting enough sleep."

"Mammy, I have saved 285 pounds and I only need 100 more. I want to go see Lisa. I really do, Mam! I'm not doing that bad in school and you said if I saved my money I could go!" I responded in a very emotional, almost crying voice. I knew this was a big decision and if she said no at that moment, I was never going to go. I pleaded my case with her and she saw my determination and the passion in my eyes.

Eventually, she said, "I will honour what I said, darling. You are very driven and I am not going to stop you. Your Daddy will be beside himself, but my word to you is my word. You save the money and then you can go."

"Ahhh... Mammy! Thanks. I love you, Mam."

"Okay, Luv, slow down…" Mam said.

"I will need to speak with Lisa's parents, make sure that everything is good with them and they will pick you up at the ferry. I will drop you off, but they need to be there to pick you up."

"Ok Mammy!" I happily agreed, " I will write Lisa a letter tonight and I'll ask her if you can call them."

"Okay, luv, that's fine," she replied.

I could not believe I had just had that conversation with Mammy. I felt respected in my work ethic and I had a very raw understanding of who my Mam really was. I knew she did not think I would save all that money to go and I was relieved that she would have to explain to my Daddy that I was going.

Wow! I am going to England!

The day finally came for me to go to visit Lisa in England. I spent all night washing my clothes, scrubbing the obvious stains on them and waiting for them to dry by the fire. The next morning, I was up early, packed and waiting in the kitchen.

Everyone in the house was asleep and then I heard Mam and Dad make noise through the kitchen ceiling as they got up out of their bed. It was a quiet, calm breakfast. Not many words were said, but I didn't feel like it was awkward or upsetting. It was just quiet.

Mammy and Daddy drove me to the Ferry in Rosslare, County Wexford. The drive to Rosslare was just over four hours and the ferry was leaving at 3:00 pm. We got there in plenty of time and Mam and Dad walked onto the ship with me and took me to the ticket counter.

"Hello," Mammy said, greeting the woman at the ticket counter.

"Good afternoon to you," she replied nicely.

"My daughter Alicia is traveling on her own and we would just like to make sure everything is on time, as her friend is picking her up at Holyhead."

"Everything is as scheduled, Ma'am. She will have a four hour voyage and it should dock in Holyhead this evening around 7:00 pm, just in time for supper," she answered.

"Lovely. Thank you very much, Ma'am," Mammy said.

We got my "walk-on" ticket and Mam and Dad walked me as far as they could. Mammy held my hand the whole way. She grabbed my shoulders, turned me to face her, looked directly into my eyes and said, "Right. We'll let you go here, luv. Have a lovely time and do not forget your manners. Always say please and thank you and mind yourself, luv. Here is an extra ten quid so you can get something to eat on the ferry. Please be careful over there, Alicia, and give Delores a quick ring to let us know you are safe."

"I will Mammy. I will do all of that, I promise."

Daddy opened his arms for a hug and I squeezed him tight. "Be a good girl, Lysh. I love you, use your wits," he said as he tapped me on the back.

"I will, Daddy, I promise. I love you."

Mammy came and hugged me tight, kissed me on the lips as she always did and said, "I love you, baby." I could tell she was going to worry about me, but I knew she would be fine.

I found my way up to the top deck and waved to Mammy and Daddy as the ship was setting sail. They stayed there the whole time, waving at me until I could not see them anymore. I was so excited to finally be on my way to England. I felt so giddy inside. My cabin was a shared cabin with four bunk beds in it. I put my stuff on one of the beds and decide to go walk around the ship.

As I made my way back upstairs, I started feeling very nauseous. I got up to the main deck and I could not walk in a straight line with the ship swaying back and forth so much. The Irish Sea was exceptionally rough that day. I ended up being so seasick I could not eat or drink anything the entire time. I just threw up and laid down the entire trip. I was so relieved when the Captain made an announcement that we would be docking in an hour. I had to find the strength to get up and give myself a quick wash so I didn't smell like I'd thrown up for the entire trip. We docked and I walked off the ship. I followed the other people. We all had to walk through a gate with two guards standing at attention.

As I walked through the gates, I immediately saw Lisa! She was running towards me with her arms wide open. We hugged each other as if we were family. It was so nice. She was so pretty. She introduced me to her twin sister Sara and her mother Sue. I felt so important to them. It was such a nice feeling.

As we went through our holiday together, Lisa created a scrapbook for me. Every place we went, she would write a memory, take a picture or stick something from there in the book. She put a packet of salt from McDonalds in there, as well as a beer coaster from the local pub. It was a great memory scrapbook to remind me of our time together.

I felt such a sense of independence being in England. I wish I'd grown up in a house like Lisa and Sara with my own room and all the modern conveniences (including central heat!) They even had their own bathrooms! Even the McDonald's Big Macs were so much better than the Burger Bite burgers. Everything felt liberating and free in England. Nobody was looking out their net curtains at you judging if you had combed your hair or if you were wearing something not Catholic-appropriate.

I was only fifteen, but I felt like I was eighteen and I could do anything. Lisa and Sara's parents were not strict like mine were. They would let us go out to pubs and off shopping, whatever we wanted to do. Lisa's boyfriend Clive had a car and we were allowed to drive anywhere with him. I could not imagine my Mammy and Daddy allowing me to go off gallivanting with a boy in a car like that.

After a couple of months, it was time for me to go home. I wanted nothing more than to stay with them forever, but obviously I couldn't. I had to go back home to dreary old Ireland, with damp growing on the walls, drafty windows and frosty mornings in bed waiting for Daddy to get the fire going before I got up.

I made the long journey back and it was about as eventful as the trip over, feeling seasick, green at the gills and nauseated. I was just sick and laid down the whole time. I couldn't even keep a cup of tea down, it was that bad.

After experiencing England, I felt the bug--the traveling bug. I saw what life was like outside of Ireland and I loved the experience of traveling and seeing how other people live. There are different cultures, different lifestyles and different rituals...just different everything, and I wanted to see it all! I want to experience more. It was only two or three weeks after arriving back home from England that I decided I wanted more traveling.

My Aunty Marie, aka Aunty Mimi, Mammy's older sister, lived in the city of Brest, France. Aunty Mimi would travel home every summer to Foynes for a couple of months and bring her kids Coco and David. She and Coco had just moved back to Ireland and Mammy mentioned that Aunty Mimi was going back to France for the summer the next year.

My ears perked up. "Mammy, do you think I can go over with them for the summer?" I asked immediately.

"Alicia, you need to stop. You were just in England, and there are plenty of children who don't get to go anywhere."

"But Mam, why can't I go? I can save my money again and I will be with Aunty Marie, so you don't have to worry. Please Mam, please? It will help me with my French class in school, too," I shamelessly added.

"Alicia, I don't want to discuss this now. I will talk to your

Father later and we will see what he says about it."

Her words were so stern I thought there was no hope of me going.

That evening, Daddy walked in from work and I ran over to him and gave him a hug and immediately sucked up to him. "Daddy do you want a cup of coffee?"

"What does she want now, Miriam?" he asked Mammy, seeing through my bullshit.

"I will talk to you about it later, Hughie," Mam replied.

I couldn't wait that long…

"Daddy, Aunt Mimi and Coco are going back to France in the summer for three months. I asked Mammy if I saved my money again could I go?" I exclaimed.

He looked at my Mammy for a moment, looked back at me, than finally said, "Miriam, I suppose if Marie is going, Alicia will be fine."

After a quick disapproving glance in my direction, Mammy replied, "All right, Hughie, she is your daughter, too."

"Ahhh, seriously? Thank you Dad! I love you!!" I shouted and gave him a great big hug.

"What about your Mother?" Daddy said.

"Oh yeah! I love you too, Mammy."

I kissed them both and ran out of the kitchen.

I couldn't believe it! I thought it would be a whole argument. They were allowing me to go to France! I ran over to Nana's house to see if Coco was there and she was. I told her I was going and she was so happy. "We are going to have a fecken blast, Lysh."

Nana was sitting by the fire and I saw her face light up when Coco and I were holding our hands together, jumping up and down.

"Alicia, that is wonderful. I hope you make the most of it, luv," she said genuinely.

"Of course I will Nan, sure. Don't I always make the best of things?" I said half-jokingly.

"Yes you do. You have that drive inside you that I wish I'd listened to when I was your age. It makes me happy to see you follow your dreams and listen to your inside voice," she replied.

I didn't think anything more about it. I was just so excited

to have Mammy and Daddy's permission to go to France. Oh, how

I loved to travel! Then it dawned on me--I had to save the money.

Aunty Mimi said I could just pay her 85 pounds for the ferry over.

She had to pay for the car anyway and they charge less per person

if you are paying for a car.

I had done it once before, so I knew I could save the

money. I had my job at Burger Bite and I was still making dinner

for the Dublin Lads. If didn't spend a penny starting now I could

have a couple of hundred pounds by the summer, easily!

I was so fecken excited. *I'm going to France like!* I

managed to save 165 pounds, but I told Mammy and Daddy that I

had 250. I gave my Aunty Mimi her 85 pounds and that left me

with 80 pounds for three months.

The day came and we packed up the Peugeot and headed

off to Cork to catch the ferry to Roscoff in France. I was worried I

would get seasick, but at least I wouldn't be alone this time. Coco and I were very close in age.

I was sixteen and she was fifteen, almost sixteen. We were very into lads at that age. Everything was about boys. The voyage was so much calmer than traveling to England. I felt a bit queasy but was not throwing up. We got settled in to our cabin and then it was time for Coco and me to roam around the ship. We had sixteen hours to sail and we were excited to see if there was a swimming pool onboard. We walked around for a bit, bought a Coke and a packet of crisps and sat in the cafeteria.

It wasn't long before Coco pointed out two handsome lads who were sitting a few tables away. "Lysh, buachaills at your nine o'clock," she said, all excited like. Buachaill is Gaelic for the word boy. Coco was trying to be cool. I turned my head discreetly and spotted them. Right at that very moment, they spotted us too.

"Shit, Coco they saw me looking right at them," I said, thoroughly mortified.

"Don't look now, but they are headed this way," she said.

"Shit, shit, shit! I look like a two-bit hooker, Coco!"

"Well, how's the goin' girls?" one of them asked.

"Can we share the table with ye?" the other one added.

"Didn't ye have yer own perfectly fine table over there?" I asked. Coco kicked me under the table and said, "Of course ye can, lads. Don't mind her. She thinks she's funny sometimes."

The two boys sat down. They were very cute. They were two brothers from County Tipperary and they were traveling to visit their Uncle in France. The oldest boy's name was Conor and the younger one was Kenneth. Conor was tall and had blue eyes and short, dirty-blonde hair. Kenneth was shorter and his hair was a bit shaggy from the lack of a haircut. They were very funny. The four of us got on very well. We had decided to meet later that evening in the cafeteria and grab some food.

Coco and I went back to the cabin and got all dolled up. Aunty Mimi knew there was something going on. "Why are ye putting eye-liner on? Did ye meet some lads or something?"

"We did. They are brothers from Tipperary," I said.

Aunty Mimi just laughed and said, "It will be an interesting voyage, then." And so it was.

We all met up later that evening and grabbed some chips and burgers.

Afterward, Kenneth said, "Let's go explore the ship, lads!"

We went into every authorized--and for that matter, unauthorized--corner of the ship. It was a lot of fun hanging out with them. We ended up playing hide and seek. I was hiding on the top deck behind some stacked blue chairs and Conor came up behind me and yelled, "Boo!" He scared the living shit out of me. I screamed and turned around and put my hands on his shoulders. He leaned in and started kissing me. I liked it, so I kissed him back. We pulled out one of the blue long recliner chairs and laid down on it together. We shifted for about twenty minutes. Ahh...he was a lovely kisser! I could have shifted him all night!

"Lads where are ye?" we heard from around the corner. It was Coco.

"Over here, Co," I yelled back.

They turned the corner, and well, if it wasn't Coco and Kenneth in front of us, holding hands. They saw us lying on the recliner chair and they started laughing.

"Well, ye are getting to know each other, too," Kenneth said. "Indeed we are!" Conor replied. Coco and I had the biggest grins on our faces as we looked at each other.

The four of us hung out until about 1:00 am in the morning. My lips were red from shifting for ages. I guess being distracted by the lads helped me cure my seasickness! Finally, it was time to say goodnight. We wrote our addresses down on a piece of paper so we could write to each other after we returned from France.

Coco and I tried to sneak into the cabin where Aunty Mimi was sleeping, or so we thought...

"Jesus, Mary and Joseph!" she exclaimed as we entered. "If this is how the summer is going to go, I will need hair dye to get rid of the all gray hairs ye are giving me. We are docking at 6:30 am in the morning. Now get into bed with ye!" Aunt Mimi ordered sternly. Coco and I felt so giddy and proud of ourselves for shifting the two boys that we didn't care what she was saying.

That summer we mostly stayed in their apartment just outside the city of Brest. It was on the second floor of a residential apartment building. We used to make spaghetti and put butter and soy sauce in it almost every day for lunch.

One day Aunty Mimi was going to Ploudalmezeau to visit her sister-in-law Danielle, so Coco and I knew we had a day to ourselves. Coco ran into the bedroom, shut the door and whispered, "Lysha, I just took 500 francs from my mother's purse!"

"You did not. Will she notice, Co?"

"No, she won't. She had a lot of cash in there."

"So what are we going to do with it, Coco?"

"Well, you are sixteen, Lysh. You can buy beer here in France."

"Grand job! We can't bring it back here. Where can we go to drink it?"

We have a storage area in the basement and the keys are hanging up by the front door."

We waited for Aunty Mimi to leave. We ran to the balcony and saw her drive off.

"Whoo-hoo, she's gone, let's go, Lysh!" Coco said, all

excited like.

We got our shoes on. Coco grabbed the cellar storage keys and we walked down to the village and into the grocery store. We picked up a twelve-pack of Brigand beer and came back to the apartment building. We went straight down to the cellar and Coco unlocked their storage area. We got a couple of boxes and sat on them with the twelve-pack of beer in between us.

We were having such a great time drinking beer and smoking fags. We got into fits of laughing and then spells of crying and we ended up hugging, saying we were sisters for life. We had the best time down in the cellar just getting fecken plastered!

This next part is a bit blurry, but I think we were down there for a good four hours, because once the beer was gone we realized Aunty Mimi said she would be home around five pm to make some dinner.

"Oh Fuckit, Lysh. I'm paralytic!" Coco said as she was trying to stand up. She put her hand out and her body started moving sideways toward the wall. I fell to the ground, I was laughing so hard at her.

Okay, so picture this: You know when someone is drunk and they turn their head to look at you, but their head turns too far and they have to correct it and turn it halfway back to find you? That's what she was like. Plus, she had this huge grin on her face the whole time. She tried to stand using the doorframe and couldn't support her weight and just fell over. I laughed so hard tears were rolling down my face and my tummy muscles hurt.

"You try getting up, smart arse!" she said.

"Fine," I said confidently. I stood up perfectly straight. Then I proceeded to trip over the box that she'd been sitting on. I was closer to the door, at least. Coco put out her hand to help me, as she was still holding on to the doorframe, and helped me up.

Now we were both vertical. All we had to do was make our way to the elevator and hit the second-floor button, walk down the hall and open the apartment door. We could do that.

We barely managed it. It took about three or four minutes to unlock the door, but we did it. We were in!

The whole apartment was spinning, though, and I could not read the clock. "What time is it, Coco?"

"Oh sweet mother of God, Lysha, its 5:15 pm. Mum will be home any minute!" She still had that big grin on her face. We went down to the bedroom and I needed to change my knickers. I was laughing so hard I had peed my pants. Fact! I flopped down face-first on the bed and then we heard the front door opening.

"Shit, she's home," I said, kind of loudly.

"Shushhhh! She will hear you. You go distract her while I sober up in the shower. Okay?" Coco whispered back to my shouting.

"Okay. I'll go distract her while you go shower and sober up," I said as I was getting up from the bed. I went to the bedroom door but then turned around and said, "Hey, why can't I go shower to sober up and you distract her?"

"Because she likes you and she will fuckin have my guts for garters and kill me!"

"Oh, right so," I said. With a mission to go distract Aunty

Mimi,

I walked down the hallway and turned the corner.

"Hello luv, how was yer day today?" she asked as she turned around to look at me.

I saw her face drop as she looked at me up and down. Right at that moment the room decided to spin again and I could not help it this time--I had to throw up, like right then and there.

I ran to the balcony, leaned over and projectile vomited all over the stucco. I could not hold it in. It was completely involuntary! It was all running down, dropping into the neighbor's balcony. Aunty Mimi was so furious.

"Oh God, I'm so sorry, Aunty!"

"What the fuck did ye do today? Where is Coco?" she yelled, her face a bright red.

"She is in the shower right now." By the time I finished my sentence she was down banging at the bathroom door.

"Corinne, open this door right now!"

"Mum, I'm in the shower."

"I am counting to ten. Either you open it or I will!"

"Okay, Mum, I'm getting out now."

Coco opened the bathroom door. She looked like a drunk person who'd tried to shower to sober up. She had a towel around her, but she still had her bra and knickers on. She had forgotten to take them off. They were dripping wet. Her eye makeup was down to her chin and I swear to God, she still had the feckin grin on her face, the same drunken grin she'd had in the cellar.

Then--this was the kicker--I couldn't help it. I got a fit of laughing just looking at the state of her. Aunty Marie was so livid, and on top of that, me laughing just was like salt in the wound.

"Where did ye get the drink? And I am only going to ask ye once!"

"Alicia bought it, Mam," Coco said.

"What did you buy?"

"I bought beer, Aunty," I said with my head down, but still laughing.

"Is this what you are spending your money on, Alicia? What would your mother say I if told her right now what ye did?

She would insist you come home. I know she would. As for you Corinne, I cannot believe you. Both of you get into your room while I think about how I am going to handle this!"

I had never seen Aunty Mimi that mad before. Coco and I stayed in the room and slept straight through until the next morning when I woke with a pounding headache. We had a very slow day just watching movies in French and lying around on the couch. This was my first major hangover and it sucked! It would be a long time before I did that again.

Those months in France meant so much to me. I have great memories that fill my heart and developed more of a drive in me to keep traveling and experiencing new cultures. I couldn't wait to see where my next adventure would take me.

Once you've depleted the old era, then arrives the

Phoenix of the new one.

~ Alicia McMahon

Chapter 6

The Lonesome Boatman ~ Silent Annie

"Ah, Dear Mother of God, please don't tell me he

is missing! I don't think I can handle this."

My sister Tina and I were very close growing up in our

teenage years. It is kinda funny actually--we seemed to date best

friends, back then. She and I had an opportunity to live in the

biggest house in Foynes. It overlooked the Shannon Estuary. It was

an old 17th century, German-built three-story house. It was nothing

short of picturesque.

Tina's boss John Donnan had bought the house on the hill and then he left the country unexpectedly. He said that Tina and I could move in until the end of the summer and just stay in the house.

At this point, Ireland was in a huge recession. Companies were shutting their doors, local shops were closing and the contracts with Foynes Harbor were diminishing every week. That was the main source of employment for a lot of villages in the area. It went from three or four ships a week to maybe one a week if we were lucky. I'd say about 65% of the locals were employed by the harbor, so the impact on our economy was huge.

The locals were starting to drink in the pubs more and more, spending their dole money on beer and whiskey, drowning their sorrows and shutting out the fact that there was just no work out there. The post office would hand out dole on Thursday mornings. You could see a line of people waiting for the post office to open. Then like clockwork, the pubs would be busy on Thursday and Friday nights with the villagers spending what little they had on a couple of pints.

Tina wanted me to move in with her to the big house, but I was only sixteen. I was insistent that I move in with Tina but Mammy and Daddy were completely against it, of course. I was a pretty determined teenager and made the move into the house on the hill despite their objections.

Tina and I shared the house. Towards the end of the summer, the electricity got cut off because we weren't paying any bills while we were there. We decided to continue to stay there even after the electricity was cut off and we used candles for light. She and I used to write poems by the fire and candlelight in the front room of the house.

It had these old glass windows and French doors that opened up and overlooked the Shannon Estuary. It almost looked like a greenhouse with windows as walls. It was nestled up into the woods on an overlook. It was creepy but majestic at the same time.

The first two floors were somewhat furnished, but the top floor had nothing, only wood floors, closets and the wooden shutters inside the windows. Every room had a fireplace. The top floor had this unnerving sense about it. It was always freezing cold and the air seemed very thin. I can honestly say that anyone who walked up there commented on how it didn't feel right. It didn't help that the entire level was not renovated. It was just wood floors, big five-foot windows and bare walls.

Not long after we moved in, we decided to have a housewarming party. I think this was actually my very first party scene with beer and cider. We had about fifteen to twenty people come. We decide to have a scavenger hunt in the house and on the grounds. We hid a little picture frame of Tina and me and that's what we were all hunting for.

We split everyone into groups and the winners who found the picture frame would be able to dare another group to do something. I had Bubbles and Skinner on my team. Skinner Enright lived in #5 Woodvale and Bubbles was his cousin who lived on the main street of Foynes.

It was very funny seeing a bunch of people with everything from lighters to candles and a couple of flashlights trying to find this picture frame. We had the fire lit in the drawing room so that

was the only lit room in the house. Tina had hidden the picture

frame in one of the chimneys on the second floor and my Cousin

Pat Murphy's team found it. Pat dared my team to go up to the

third floor and sit in the middle of the room for five minutes

straight.

"Fuck off Pat. No way am I doing that," Bubbles said with

obvious distress in his voice.

"Right, so, Skinner and Lysha, off ye go," Pat said.

"In my bollox. You can keep fucken off there, Pat," said

Skinner.

"Fine! Yer all a bunch of pansies anyway," I said, as I was

walking into the house toward the first flight of stairs.

As I was making my way up the stairs, I said to myself,

"Shit, bad idea, Lysh." As I turned the corner and headed toward

the thin stairway to the top floor, the temperature changed

immediately, and I swear to you I heard a deep muted voice

coming from the top of the stairs. I stopped dead in my tracks.

Did I really hear that?

Then I could hear the groups on their way up to the second floor.

It was probably nothing.

I waited until I could see them on the landing of the second floor before I continued up to the third floor.

Then I heard Pat say, "Now, lads, ye can't talk to her. It has to be dead silent."

"Ah, Feckit!" I said to myself.

"Right, lads, start timing it now," I yelled from the gable end of the third floor.

"Gowan, you good thing," Bubbles yelled back.

I bit my lower lip, walked forward and sat directly in the center of the big room, making sure to keep the door open for a quick escape. I looked out the window and saw the moon glowing on the Shannon Estuary and I could make out the house on Foynes Island.

I can still see that picture clearly in my head today. Within a minute, I felt uneasy and very anxious. I wanted to be tough and have the spunk to pull this off, especially when the two boys couldn't. I told myself that the boys were only fifteen feet and nine stairs away from me.

"You can do this, Lysh."

About three minutes into the solitary confinement, I could tell there was a presence of something in the room with me. The air became very dense. A thick, almost smothering claustrophobic feeling surrounded me. I could not see anything, but there was something there with me. The hairs on the back of my neck stood up and I felt like I couldn't breathe.

Instantly, I knew I should not be there. I turned to look at the doorway and that's when I saw it. I am thinking of a way to describe what I saw right now for my book. The best way to explain it is that I saw something walking fast, turning a corner, with a visible misty trail behind it.

I freaked!

Well, I bolted towards the door and I think I hit every other step on the stairs. I jumped from the corner of the third-floor stairs onto the landing on the second floor. I almost took out the boys. I couldn't say a word for about ten seconds.

Then, all I said was, "Yer right, lads. Fuck that!"

I ran outside and took a swig of my cider and there was a fecken fag butt in there. I nearly swallowed it. I started gagging and I almost threw up. They all got great laugh at me, and then they decided to take it easy on me because at least I tried the dare.

So as a punishment for not doing the dare, the two boys had to go down to the road, take their shirts off and do twenty push-ups across the white line with me on their backs. All I had to do was moon the next car that came on the road.

Done!

This was my second experience with feeling a presence like that. I know for a fact there was something up there and I began to learn to trust my Crone voice and feelings more after that experience.

Tina and I used to head down to the Shannon House and play pool quite a bit. This is where we met a few boys from

Kilrush, County Clare, across the Shannon Estuary. It was a lot of fun meeting up with them and playing pool. There was Martin Peter Cusack, Mick Burke, Thomas Whelan and Fintan Griffin.

Martin Peter was about 5'6" with a strong build, dirty-blond hair and nothing but teeth when he smiled. He had a very outgoing personality and had one of the kindest, most genuine hearts you could ever meet. Mick Burke was about 6'3" with black hair, thick black beard and had a barrel of a chest. A gentle giant. He would always be there to put his arm around you if you were sad and lend an ear if you needed it. Thomas was slender, tall and kind. He's eyes were nothing short of dreamy. They would smile on their own. He was soft spoken and a true gentleman. Fintan was about 5'10", of an average build and had thick glasses. He was always up for a funny comment. He was the quiet one in the group.

Thomas's Uncle owned a tugboat company called Whelan's Tugboats and they had a contract in Foynes. They would help guide the ships in and out of the pier to load and unload.

After a while, Tina started dating Martin Peter and soon thereafter, I started dating Thomas. The boys were very funny. They would make us laugh over stupid comments. Thomas had a red sports car and nobody had anything like that in Foynes at the time. He would let me drive the car around town even though I did not have a license. I would drive his car behind him down to Kerry and across the Ferry to Clare. He would have to bring the van back to Kilrush sometimes for his father's business.

I will never forget the first time I had to drive onto the ferry. You literally have to get within inches of the car in front of you. Keep in mind all cars were manual stick not automatic. Well as long as it was Thomas in front of me, I wouldn't get in trouble if I hit the van he was driving. He was so kind and understanding.

Tina and I, Martin Peter and Thomas were always together. The boys would take the tugboat out the Shannon Estuary in the mornings. They would blow the air horn and wave at the house on the hill. Tina and I would rush to the five-foot windows and wave back at them. It is a fond memory for both Tina and me. We have talked about it a few times over the years.

One morning, I was still in bed and Tina came in to wake me to tell me the boys were waiting for their wave. I jumped out of the bed in my knickers and vest, went straight to the window and started waving to the lads in the tugboat coming down the Estuary. I was delighted I didn't miss the wave. Well, later that evening we met the boys at the Shannon House and they were all giggling away at something.

"What are ye laughing at lads? What's so funny, like?" Tina asked.

Martin Peter said, "Nice pink knickers, Lysha!"

Mick and Thomas started cracking up and Thomas said, "We should have told ye we get the binoculars out each morning to see ye wave to us through the window."

Martin Peter jumped right in and said, "Well, how r'a knicks? I wonder what colour they'll be tomorrow? Will we take bets, lads?"

"Ahh.. Feck off Martin Peter. Would you ever leave me alone, like," I replied.

They all gave me an awful time after that. It was a good month before they stopped slaggin' me about my knickers. I loved it, though, all the same.

Those were good times, just full of life. But we couldn't have foreseen the tragedies soon to come.

We all stuck together for months. We would go to Kilrush for the weekends, up the country to Galway for the Irish music festival and down to Ballybunion beach for a day trip. It became the usual suspects up for adventure having a feckin blast together. Martin Peter even bought Tina a promise ring in Galway! He was proud as punch to call her his girlfriend. They were always holding hands. He adored the ground she walked on. Everyone said they were great together. It was lovely to witness.

Mick would always make everyone laugh out loud, even when he didn't mean to. He just had that wit about him.

Then Thomas, well, he was the fella with the car. It would

be Thomas driving, me in the front seat, Tina, Martin Peter and Mick Burke all strapped in the back of the car.

I'll never forget this one time we were driving back to Limerick from the Galway music festival. It was torrential rain and very blustery that evening. We were all packed into the car and Mick Burke grabbed the front seat of Thomas's car, so I piled in the back with Tina and Martin Peter.

It was a long weekend of partying and drinking so we were all tired in the back seat. I was just about to fall asleep and put my head on Tina's shoulder when all of a sudden Mick and Thomas rolled down all the windows in the car and it was fecken freezing. We were getting drenched to the bone. The two boys had the heater blaring on them in the front seat and us, the three stooges in the back, were freezing cold and getting drenched. We screamed at them for a good couple of miles. I'll never forget it--they had **Bohemian Rhapsody** blaring on the radio to wash out our screams in the back. We were well awake for the rest of the drive home after that.

After a few months, Tina and Martin Peter started to fight a bit. Thomas and I found ourselves spending less time with them because they were not getting along. It had been a few weeks and I noticed Tina was being very quiet about it and not wanting to go down for a pint that often.

One day I was walking down from the house on the hill into the village to hit up #8 for food because I was starved. As I walked past the Shannon House, there was Tina and Martin Peter sitting in the beer garden in front. I could tell by Tina's face something was up. I walked over to them and said, "How's it goin', lads?"

Tina got up from her seat and said, "Well, that's it then, I will go to Mammy's with you Lysh." Tina had just broken up with Martin Peter. It was obvious he was devastated.

"Tina, please don't do this, we are meant to be together, PLEASE!" He screamed at Tina.

"Keep walking, Lysh. Don't look back at him," Tina leaned over and whispered to me.

She walked with me the rest of the way to Mammy's house. It was a quiet walk there. Everyone was surprised to hear the news that they'd broken up. Thomas felt so bad for Martin Peter. He said he had never seen him so heartbroken before.

Martin Peter turned to the drink hard--very hard, actually. All he did after work was go to the Shannon House and get plastered every single day. And forget about the weekends--it was all day in the pub, and this continued week after week. My heart went out to him. He was just truly heartbroken.

Thomas and I were still going strong. Mammy and Daddy had bought a house in Mount David, Shanagolden and moved out of #8. They ended up selling #8 to my Uncle Finbar. Tina and I decided to move out of the house on the hill because people kept coming around looking for the owner and their money. So we migrated up to the new house in Mount David. There is only so much you can do in a house in the woods with no electricity.

It was just a few weeks after Tina and Martin Peter broke up when Thomas arrived up at Mount David pretty early in the morning. I heard his car drive up the stone driveway and come to a quick stop. I thought he'd come up for a cup of tea and some breakfast. He came in the front door and I heard him walk straight down the hallway to my bedroom.

"Wake up Lysh, wake up! Martin Peter is missing," he said, panting from sheer panic.

"Ah, Jesus, Thomas, you're joken me, aren't' you?" I said.

"I'm not joken, Lysh. I wish I was! Nobody has seen him since Friday and he didn't show up for work, so I checked his bunk on the tug and it hasn't been touched since Friday."

"Maybe he hitchhiked to the ferry and went to his Dad's house in Kilrush?"

"He would have told me, or even asked me to drive him there."

A couple of days went by and Thomas said he was going to take the ferry and see if he was at home in Kilrush.

"Lysh, I need to make sure he is all right. I have a feeling about this, and it's not good."

"Grand, so, Thomas. I'll go with you," I said.

We drove to Kerry and caught the ferry to Clare and then drove to Kilrush. We went straight to Martin Peters' Dad's house and there was no sign of him. We went to the local pub and they said the last time they'd seen Martin Peter was a couple of months earlier when we were all there together.

Now we were extremely worried. We went back to Foynes that afternoon and reported him missing to the Garda. They formed a search party for the shores and a dive crew in the harbor. We searched a few miles along the rocky shores for days and days.

The next Saturday morning, Daddy and Thomas got up very early to join the search crew. Half the village was down there. I got up around nine o'clock and went into the kitchen to put the kettle on. I was going to fill a flask of hot tea and then bring it down to the harbor for Daddy and Thomas. I was just on my way to wake Tina and get dressed when Thomas walked in the door.

I took one look at Thomas's face and I knew something bad had happened.

"Thomas, what's going on?"

"We found him, Lysh. He's dead! He must have fallen into the pier trying to jump onto the tugboat after his night of boozen," Thomas said with his head down.

I felt like someone had punched me in the stomach. I was sick.

"What? What? You cannot be serious, Thomas. No, no, no!" I was screaming.

Tina ran into the room. She knew it! I saw her face turn white in front of my eyes. Her legs wobbled underneath her. She was beside herself. I ran forward and grabbed her. I ended up holding her for about five minutes and we just cried our eyes out.

Once we had calmed down enough, Thomas told us the details. He said it was hard to recognize him because the body was so bloated from being in the water, but it was him. He had his leather jacket on that Tina had bought him for his birthday and his Celtic ring on his finger. Ah, Mother of God…our Martin Peter was dead.

The entire community was devastated and overcome with grief. Tina was inconsolable and blamed herself for a long time. I saw pure heartache and sorrow in her eyes. She became numb and distant emotionally.

Soon after, we all went to Kilrush for his funeral. Half the village of Foynes was there, including my family, and of course all of his friends--the Kilrush boys, Thomas, Mick and Fintan.

Mick paid tribute to Martin Peter by playing **The Lonesome Boatman** on the tin whistle. This song is powerful and is known by all sailors around Ireland. When Mick was playing it in the church, you could have heard a pin drop, it was so reflective and profound. There was a feeling other than sadness there. It was truly mystical and spiritual.

After the funeral, we all headed to the local pub in Kilrush for a quick pint and then everyone headed back to Foynes and into the Shannon House for a wake of sorts. We sang, remembered, smiled and cried. There were stories told, poems read and songs sung. Mick recited *Silent Annie,* a poem written to **The Lonesome Boatman** tune, by the fire to a quiet somber crowd. The whole pub raised their drinks in hand and paid homage to our dear friend.

It took a long time for all of us to process the loss of our amazing friend. We kept his memory and spirit with us.

After a few months, something happened between Tina and Mick. I think they took comfort in each other and mourned together. Mick was so concerned for Tina. He did everything he could to comfort her.

After a while, Mick ended up asking Tina out officially and then they were a bonified item. Mick cherished Tina and Tina needed that from Mick. They looked so happy together. We kept up our usual routine with meeting the boys and going back to Kilrush with them the odd weekend, so they could see their families. Thomas, Mick and Fintan still stayed on the tugboat during the week because they would need to start work early. Some weekends they would end up crashing at our house in Mount David because we would have a few beers and sit by the fire all

121

night.

The boys were becoming part of the community as well-respected, hardworking, good, sound men. Mammy and Daddy loved them all. We would all have dinner together in Mount David, as well as Christmas, birthdays, etc.

Mick was very happy. I think he felt as if he belonged. He looked after all of us as if we were his own family. He would shower Tina with gifts all the time. He would do anything for her. He just fit right in with our family.

A few months after the funeral, maybe a year, Tina and Mick were not as happy as they had been earlier in their relationship. I saw Tina withdraw more and more and I didn't know why. They were arguing more frequently and then eventually, they broke up.

They were both hurt. I think they realized they were a comfort to each other after losing someone they had loved. They both turned to drink for a while. I noticed Tina was hitting the sauce big time.

She'd used to drink Pernot, which was a liqueur that tasted like black licorice. She would drink in the Shannon House and Mick would hit up the Foynes Inn, so they would not run into each other while on a session or a night out. Mick made many attempts to get Tina back, but it never happened.

It was a few months later, I can't remember exactly how long, when Mick went missing. Mick did not show up for work and nobody could find him. We all thought the same thing--Jesus Christ Almighty, not again! Please, Lord, let there be some sort of explanation for this!

I called Tina and asked her if she had seen Mick lately.

"Ah, Dear Mother of God, please don't tell me he is missing! I don't think I can handle this," she said.

This was so surreal it was a complete deja-vu moment.

After a few days with Mick not showing up for work, they launched another search and rescue.

Mick Burke's body was found floating just south of where Martin Peter's body was discovered in the Shannon Estuary.

Mick Burke was dead.

They think the same thing happened to Mick as did to Martin Peter, drunk and trying to make the step from the pier to the tugboat and probably falling in between the boat and the pier. This was an extraordinary coincidence, almost unfathomable at the time.

Was this really happening again?

Mick's Funeral was held in the same village church in Kilrush as Martin Peter.

Needless to say, there was not one person at that time that offered to play **The Lonesome Boatman** at Mick's funeral or read *Silent Annie* by the pub fire. My Uncle Seamus did, however, later put into words what we all felt. Mick had such a positive effect on so many people. He was such a good person and a loving friend. Our real-life gentle giant had left this world.

I didn't know how to deal with this emotionally. I felt robbed of beautiful memories and felt so empty, almost like two brothers had been taken from our family. Who was going to make fun of what color of knickers I was wearing? Who was going to put a warm, strong arm around us when we were sad?

Who?

I was very worried about Tina's emotional state. Not only did she have to process this unbelievable occurrence herself, but she also had to deal with some cruel rumors that started circulating around the surrounding small villages and towns. There was even one about her being a black widow and another one, *The curse of Tina Mc*.

It was just so sad. My poor, poor sister. She went into a deep depression after that. She was so afraid to even go outside the door. The whole community was in shock. I wanted to protect her from all the mean judgmental and small-minded people, but she just had to give it time.

Losing my dear friends had a huge impact on my being, in my heart, in my entire existence. Life is so precious, it's an absolute gift, and it's a privilege.

I found myself wondering, *What is life overall?* Is it a

particular instance in time? Is it a feeling in a moment? Is it to have an impact or impression on someone else?

What is life?

I wanted to go and live my life outside of the village and explore other cultures. This urge would stay with me until I actually listened and eventually followed it.

Below is a poem my Uncle Seamus wrote about Mick soon after his passing.

"To most of us the real life is the life we do not lead."
~ Oscar Wilde

A Tragic Waste

(A Tribute to Mick Burke)

I stand beside this peaceful Grave, In Carrigaholt in County Clare,

And No! I do not stand-alone; there are many people here.

Some of them I know quite well, I can also see my Brother,

Most are total strangers, who seem to know each other.

A massive array of colour, Flowers, Bouquets at their best,

Mark this spot, this final bed where Mick is laid to rest.

The prayers are said, the Priest has gone but no one is in haste.

Their thoughts must be the same as mine. God! What a tragic

waste.

My thoughts drift back o'er pleasant times, in Foynes, as I recall.

When I first set eyes on this bearded lad, well over six feet tall.

At least that's how he seemed to me, a giant to behold,

But beneath that bulk of jet black hair there beat a heart of gold.

He was rugged and was handsome, in a very manly way,

He was also very gifted as I later learned that day.

In a session, one of many, in the Shannon House that night,

When the crack it was almighty and the atmosphere just right.

Mike Fitzsimons got out his guitar and Phil Nolan rosined his bow,

A Filipino tried to sing a song, who asked him no one knows.

To say the man could sing at all would be so very wrong.

What saved us was when someone roared, "Mick Burke to sing a song!"

He sang, "I'm going to Love You Forever," then Cat Stevens, "Father and Son,"

The voice of this strapping young seaman applauded by everyone.

Then someone produced a tin whistle, don't anyone ask me from where,

But it passed from one hand to another 'till it reached young Michael from Clare.

My God I'll never forget it when he put this tin tube to his lips.

The tune that he played was pure magic, held the audience complete in his grip.

It was called the "Lonesome Boatman" I'd heard it played in the past,

This time it is locked in my memory and will stay for as long as I last.

'Twill remind me of good times together, how we bullshit while having a jar,

When we talked of the places we'd been to, reminiscing on places afar.

'Twill remind me of a young man so virile, wanting naught but simplicity in life.

Like a pint, a good craic and some music. No battles, no hunger, no strife.

'Twill remind me of a Lad on the river, his tanned face facing the sun,

Getting on with his job on the Tugboat, respected by everyone.

'Twill remind me of Fintan and Eolan, and of how this gang all begun,

We must also remember young Martin, now both of them, sadly, are gone.

'Twill remind me of the chapel, this morning, as I heard it played once more,

It brought a teardrop to my eye, it never did before,

I saw so many people stand and weep, saw hardened menfolk

quiver,

Some from places far away, some from both sides of the river.

My thoughts go to his Mum and Dad and that's what Mick would

want,

To brother Pat and sisters and those Mick held in fond,

As I stand upon this peaceful place, head bowed in silent prayer,

Saying, "God Bless Mick but not goodbye, someday we'll all meet

there."

As I stand upon this peaceful grave, still no one is in haste,

I turn my eyes to heaven, "God, what a tragic Waste."

Author ~ Seamus Murphy

"One never knows why things happen in life, but my
memories are mine to own"

~ Alicia McMahon

Chapter 7

My Destiny Called and I Answered

"Daddy stood there and waved until we drove out of the yard. I looked back at him and I knew his heart was breaking."

Thomas's uncle lost the contract for the tugboats with the harbor in Foynes due to the recession. Thomas needed to find another job. He had an aunt in England who said she would give him a place to stay until he found a job. Thomas asked me if I wanted to go with him and find work over there.

I could not find work in Ireland for the life of me. I had

looked everywhere. Daddy used to deliver oil for Estuary Fuel and he would have regular runs down to Cork, up to Wexford--all over the place, really. I would catch a ride down to Cork with Daddy and look for work while he was unloading the fuel a few towns away and then he would pick me up after a few hours. I had no money and my boyfriend was considering moving to England for work. So I decided I was going with him and we would both look for work and get a flat over in London.

This took quite a bit of convincing with both families. Thomas was nineteen and I was seventeen. I did need permission from Mammy and Daddy. I was very strong-willed and pushed the working issue with them. Plain and simple, I needed a job. I needed to leave the hurt and sadness after losing my friends. I had to find my way.

After a few conversations, they reluctantly agreed to it.

Once I got approval to move to England, I went down to Nana's and I told her the news.

I was a little surprised by her response. I thought she would give me a few words of advice and good hug and kiss and then send me on my way. But she didn't. She talked about when her kids decided to fly the coop and go to England for work and what impact that had on her.

"Are you sure you want to do this, luv?" she asked almost nonchalantly.

"I do, Nan. I can't find work anywhere. I need to start my life outside of the village."

"Well, you have the drive and determination in you already, so you have my blessing, darling," she said with a smile on her face.

"Don't worry about me, Nana, I'm going to be just fine," I said as I hugged her tightly.

"Please mind yourself, Alicia. The world is a lot different than Foynes. And listen to your inside! Please!"

Little did I know at that time how true Nana's words really were.

"I will Nan. I love the bones of you!"

We headed off and got to the airport and there was some confusion with the airline tickets. I think it was a credit card issue. My mother ended up writing a check for both tickets right then and there. I knew Mammy and Daddy didn't have the funds to be just writing a check for a couple of hundred pounds. I felt so grateful Mammy did that for me.

Off we went to England to make a life for ourselves. Thomas's Uncle Bob picked us up at the Airport. Bob was a Taxi driver. He had the big black London taxi with the doors that open arse-ways. Bob brought us to his house, where Mary was waiting with dinner on the table. Bob and Mary had two teenage sons who also lived at the house. Mary, being a strict Catholic, insisted that I sleep in the spare room, while Thomas slept on the couch.

Thomas and I didn't waste any time. We started job hunting the very next day. It took a few weeks, but Thomas found a job as a bartender in Hemel Hempstead, Herts. He worked there for a couple of weeks until he got his first paycheck, and then we moved out of Mary and Bob's and into a flat.

It was actually just an upstairs bedroom in a row house and we had to share a kitchen with two other families. I spent my time buying the local paper, circling the possibilities, using public phones, buying bus fares, chasing down each lead and finally walking into every shop and asking if they were hiring.

Then I got a message from Mary that a store called and asked for me to come in for an Interview. I went in the next day, interviewed, and got the job. I started a week later as a floor person in a boutique called Next Boutique. My main responsibility was to price the merchandise and keep the floor tidy. I was trained on the till as a backup person if need be.

Thomas and I were working every day just trying to get by. He had to work late every night and I had to go to work early in the morning, so needless to say, it was taking its toll on our relationship.

After work I would listen to Patsy Cline over and over again in that little room we rented and feel lonely and sad. Patsy Cline reminded me of my Daddy and Mammy. They would play her record on the weekend mornings.

As it got busy at the Boutique for the holidays, the upstairs manager quit, and I had to step into that role until they found someone else to take the position. I felt fantastic about it. I thought this would look great on my CV, so I didn't mind that I was not getting paid any additional money. I got very comfortable there and enjoyed the job a lot. I was managing the staff schedules and checking people out at the register, so I was always around people.

One day I went to the break room for a cup of tea and a crumpet. As I walked in the door I saw a strange person going through the employees' handbags. He looked right at me, dropped the purse and pulled out a knife. He put it to my throat and said, "You'd better not scream." He proceeded to throw me up against a metal railing and ran past me toward the back stairs.

It took me about thirty seconds to realize what had just happened. I started screaming and the other employees came running into the break room. They called the police or as they say in England, "Old Bill," and they took me down to the police station--where, I might add, they gave me a brandy for my nerves, even though they knew I was only seventeen and not eighteen.

I was pretty shaken up. My arm was swollen black and blue from the iron stairs. I felt at that moment maybe I did leave home too soon.

This was a big event for me. I went from being raised in a village of about five-hundred people to working in London. It was definitely a culture shock, to say the least.

I was terrified to be alone. I would walk to the flat after work and play Patsy Cline and Johnny Cash and just cry my eyes out all by myself, afraid to go outside on my own. I tried to overcome it and shake off my fears, but I just couldn't.

A few days later, I went to the pub where Thomas worked. I didn't want to be alone at the flat. I sat at the bar and Thomas gave me a Coke. I looked over and saw the public phone on the wall. He asked me if I had talked to my family yet and told them what had happened.

"No, no yet. I will now, so," I said. I walked over to the

phone, picked up the receiver, put four English pounds in it and called home.

"Hello?" Mammy said.

"Hi Mammy, it's me," My voice started breaking up trying to hold back my tears.

"Alicia, are you okay?" Mammy knew I wouldn't call unless something had happened.

"I'm okay, Mammy. There was an incident. I walked in on a fella stealing from the handbags in the break room at work and he put a knife to my throat and threw me to the ground and I hurt my arm," I said in one long, emotional sentence.

Then I started crying. I looked over at Thomas working behind the bar. He stared directly at me and he knew I was going to leave and go back home.

We talked about it for a few days and decided that I just needed to go home. Thomas was angry at me and I felt so sad about that because I didn't want to leave him. I wanted him to come home, too.

He decided against it and said he was staying and working. The feelings I wrestled with were tremendous. I had to go home, and yet my heart was breaking leaving Thomas. The ache inside really hurt. I didn't want to leave him, but I had to listen to what I knew I needed to do.

Go Home.

Mammy sent me more money and I got a flight home.

I got to Mount David and I didn't leave my room for about two weeks. I was depressed, crying and sad. I was in a bad state. I wasn't sure if it was the trauma from being in the robbery or if it was my heart breaking after leaving Thomas. Mammy would check in on me throughout the day and even bring me in my dinner to the bedroom. My sisters Tina and Jenny would come in and try to rally me to go out. I just was not up to doing anything. I just wanted to stay in my room and cry and be sad by myself.

This one particular day, Daddy came in with a cup of tea and a slice of toast for me.

He put them on the side table and said, "You will be fine,

Lysh, I promise. You are my daughter and you are tough! You're a Mac!"

Then he left the room and came back about two minutes later and handed me a picture. It was a passport picture of him. It was even signed on the back, "Hugh McMahon." I still have that picture in my jewelry box today.

He didn't speak a word about why he gave me a picture of himself. It was one of those humble times that didn't need a word spoken. I didn't know it then, but he was teaching me to have that manner myself. I sometimes just pass a note, rub a back, give a hug or just kiss a cheek without words. The feeling and gesture is what I want to rely on, not the words themselves. I didn't know it at the time, but Daddy's words gave me strength back then and would stay with me until I'd need them the most…in yet another land far away.

It took a while for me to snap back into reality after I returned from England and broke up with Thomas. Now it was time to pick myself up to face the feckin job hunt again. Tina and I were both back living in Mount David and we decided to see if we were eligible for the dole while we were looking for work. Jenny was working in the Shannon House at the time, so she stayed down there.

Because Tina was over eighteen, she was eligible to draw the dole. I was only seventeen at the time, so I was not able to draw the dole, but I was eligible to draw stamps from when I worked a job at Burger Bite. The stamps for me were about 26 Irish pounds a week in those days. Tina got about 42 pounds. That was enough for her and me to go buy a couple of bottles of wine on the Thursday that our dole came in, head up to Mount David and clean the house from top to bottom.

We would literally clean the windows with vinegar, water and newspaper, Hoover the floors and polish everything. We had a two-speaker boom box and played the soundtrack to **Top Gun**, blaring Kenny Loggin's **Danger Zone**. We had to keep unplugging it and carrying it to the next room we needed to clean. This became a ritual for Thursdays, with the ritual headache on Friday mornings.

Tina and I would also go play racquetball on Thursday in the community center, which was directly across from the Shannon House. We picked Thursdays because the dole money was usually gone by then and we always put a fiver away, so we could have a glass of Smithwick's and a game of pool after we played.

It was not too long before Tina and I started seeing a couple of best friends, Declan and Liam. We had known the boys for a while, but we started seeing them regularly at the Shannon House every Thursday. They knew we would be there after racquetball. They were both from Dublin and they worked at Aughinish Alumina, which is an Aluminum plant about four miles outside of Foynes on the Limerick road. Liam and Declan used to hang out with Bubbles back then, so we all knew each other. We would hang out at the Shannon House, play pool and listen to Queen's **Bohemian Rhapsody** on the jukebox. I think I resisted Liam after the whole Thomas breakup. I kept him at arm's length, for sure, but after a while, we started hanging out together more and then ultimately, we started seeing each other.

A couple of months went by and I was standing in line behind about ten people at the post office in Shanagolden waiting to draw my stamps, as the whole cleaning-house-wine-thing was getting old. I glanced at Tina behind me in the queue and said, "I am so feckin tired of this, Teen. I have to find work." Tina laughed. She threw her head back and said, "Don't we all? You and 75% of the country, Lysh. This is the worst recession in over sixty years, like."

I picked up a newspaper that very second and said, "There has to be work somewhere." Every day I walked down to the Spar supermarket in the village and bought a newspaper. Mam and Dad had a phone in Mount David at this point, so I would use the phone to call about jobs and try to set up interviews. I was relentless. I knew if I looked hard enough I would have to find something.

Then one day an ad in the newspaper caught my eye. *Be an Au Pair in America for One Year*. It was like Christmas morning for me. I am not joking--my eyes lit up and I felt so giddy.

I knew this was my destiny. I cannot explain it, but I just knew. I feckin knew!

I made sure I read the ad carefully and understood what it was saying. I actually had to read it three or four times to comprehend it. Eventually, I called the number and talked to a woman in Mallow, County Cork and she explained everything to me. I would have to go down to Cork and take a series of tests and bring a Doctor's Certificate saying I was in good health. I would have to fill out all the paperwork, get it signed by a parent and go back down for an Interview.

I announced my master plan to Mammy and Daddy that evening during dinner. It happened to be my favorite-- homemade chips, fried egg, sausage and baked beans.

I walked into the kitchen, sat down at the table with a big grin on my face and said, "Mam, I'm off to America! I found a job to be an *Au Pair* for a year. I have it all sorted and they said if I pass my physical and the written exam, I'm good to go!"

Mammy's first response was "Right so, Lysh, off to the States you go." She passed it off as if It was never going to happen.

Daddy looked right at me and said, "No you are not. Remember what happened to you in England luv. It's too soon."

"Well, I already called them, Daddy, and I have to go down to Cork and fill everything out," I said sternly.

Then Mammy looked over at me and said, "You're not jokin', are you, luv?"

"No, Mam, I'm not. I am going to the States just for a year and then I will be back."

Tina had walked into the kitchen as we were talking and said, "Lysha, what am I going to do for a feckin year?"

"I don't know, Teen, why don't you sign up, too?"

"Will you call her back and ask her if your sister can come too?" Tina asked.

"Ah, Tina, that's a brilliant idea. Let's call her in the morning," I said, all excited.

The next morning, I woke up anxious for Tina to get up.

We couldn't wait to jump on the phone and ask the lady in Cork if Tina could go to America also. I made the call and it was easy. The lady said yes! We could both interview with the company.

We had to be in Cork city at 8:30 am on Thursday the next week. We got the paperwork in the post and had it all filled out and ready. Daddy said he could take us down to Cork in his lorry because he had a delivery of oil that day in Cork, but we would need to leave the house by 5:45 am.

Tina and I woke up at 5:00 am and started to prepare for our big day. I had my blouse already ironed and ready to put on and my skirt was hanging on the clotheshorse by the fire. We were rushing around the house getting dressed, styling our hair and grabbing some toast to eat on the way.

Daddy dropped us off at 7:15 pm on the main road into Cork city and said he would be back at the same spot to pick us up at 1:00 pm. We did not have cell phones back then, so we had to make sure we were there if we wanted a ride back to Limerick.

We found the building where the interviews were being

held but they were not open yet. We walked two buildings down to the bakery and just sat there drinking tea until it was time for our appointments.

I was called in to interview first. It took about an hour. Tina was waiting, just sitting on a chair outside the interview room. The lady was very nice. I gave her my paperwork and she went through it with me. She saw I was already certified in CPR and she was happy about that. I had to take a test on childminding and I passed it with flying colours. It was not that bad, actually.

After the test she read my answers, stood up and put her hand out to shake mine. "Well, congratulations, Alicia, you have passed all the necessary requirements to become an *Au Pair* with us. I will let you know when we have a family for you."

Holy shit, I couldn't believe it! I did it! My insides were shaking with the excitement of it all. I felt nothing short of elated.

Tina was called in right as I was leaving so I couldn't tell her what to expect. I sat and waited for her to finish. It only took her about forty-five minutes. She came out of the interview room with the biggest smile I had seen on her face in over a year. She'd been accepted, too!

We walked out of the building and Tina said, "Right. Let's celebrate. We need to find a pub!"

"You don't need to tell me twice, Teen," I said.

We both had a glass of Smithwick's and we shared a ham and cheese sandwich. Then it was time to go meet Daddy and tell him the good news!

Tina and I spent the next few weeks getting all our ducks in a row and all the paperwork in order. We both got approved and got our packets on our host families in America. Tina was twenty-one years old and she got three children for a single Dad just outside of Albany, New York. I was assigned three children for a family in Stratford, Pennsylvania, just outside of Philadelphia.

This was a very exciting time for me. I said to myself, "You did it, Lysh! You knew you would find a job!"

Now we had to prepare to go to America for a year. Tina and I did our best to pack accordingly. We could only take two bags for a year, so we did what we could.

The agency gave us the trip details and had us take a train from Limerick City to Dublin City. We had to be at the train station in the city by 4:30 pm, so we got up with Daddy early that morning and he made us a big Irish fry up. He made lovely Irish sausages, eggs, rashers, black and white pudding, fried tomatoes and soda bread.

Daddy had to go to work by 6:30 am, so we had our time with him at breakfast. There was an unusual calmness about that morning. Daddy was very quiet, as were Tina and I, which is unusual in itself. There was not a whole lot to be said. Sometimes there is no need. As Daddy was getting up he started clearing off the plates and cups from the table.

"Jesus Christ, Daddy, we will do that. Go on now. You will be late for work," Tina said.

"Grand, so. Listen, ye be careful in America and mind yerselves," he said.

He gave us a hearty hug and left the kitchen.

I ran after him and asked, "Daddy, what time will you be

reloading the lorry at the yard today?"

"About half-one, Lysh," he replied.

"Right, sure, we will swing by there to say goodbye around half-one, so," I said.

"Grand," Daddy said closing the front door.

Tina was standing behind me and gave me a puck in the shoulder and said, "Now you just made it worse."

"What do you mean, Tina?" I asked, genuinely puzzled.

"He would have just rather say his goodbye here, Lysh. Daddy does not deal with these things well," she replied.

"How did I know, like? It didn't feel right, Teen. It wasn't a proper goodbye."

After breakfast we did our rounds to say goodbye to everyone in Woodvale. That was an unwritten rule with the entire Murphy Clan. You had to do your rounds to everyone, and nobody leaves to go anywhere without Nana's goodbye and blessing. That's just the way it was.

Nan told us that she was coming in to the city with us and

she would see us off at the train station. We were delighted.

Now we had to head over to Estuary Fuel to catch Daddy while he was reloading the fuel tank on his lorry. As Tina and I turned into the pier on our way to see him, we both had lumps in our throats and I felt sick to my stomach.

"Lysha, we need to keep this quick in and out and don't arse around, okay?" Tina said to me.

We made our way down the pier and turned into the Estuary Fuel yard and there was Daddy's lorry being fueled. We saw him get out of the lorry. Tina and I both got out and calmly waited by the car. I watched him walk across the yard toward us, he seemed very calm and he had those aviator mirror sunglasses on.

I couldn't wait until he reached us, so I ran over to him and hugged him tight. He allowed it for about five seconds and then started the tap on the back--you know, the okay, we are done tap. I said, "I love you, Daddy. I will miss you." He didn't say anything back to me. I saw a tear slipping from under his aviator glasses. Tina stepped in and did the same. I followed her lead as she turned towards the car.

Dad stood there and waved until we drove out of the yard. I looked back at him and I knew his heart was breaking, watching us drive away that day. He has a very soft heart with a tough exterior. It must have been hard to watch two of his girls head off to another continent for an entire year.

Tina and I had a good cry in the car and headed into the Shannon House to say goodbye to Jenny, then up to Mount David for our bags.

So we packed up the Nissan Blue Bird and headed off up the road.

Mammy and Nana were in front and Tina, Kim, Amy and I were in the back seat. Kim was six years old and Amy was five. I looked at them and thought, *I'm going to miss a whole year of them growing up.* I looked at Amy and I noticed she had tears streaming down her cheeks. I put my arm around her and asked, "What's wrong, baby girl?"

"I will miss ye both very, very much," she replied in her

soft voice. Not being able to pronounce her *V*''s, it sounded more like, "I will miss ye both bery, bery much."

I was so impressed with her poise and being so humble at five years old. I remember thinking to myself that she was either extremely wise for a five year old or she had been here before.

I could tell that Mammy was beside herself. She was very quiet the whole drive into the city. Nana was doing most of the talking, imparting wisdom on us, like to make sure we always wore clean knickers in case we were in an accident and to always keep our Mammy's phone number with us in case of emergency. She covered everything.

We pulled up to Limerick Train Station with not much time to spare. We unloaded the bags and went to find our train. I was leading the group as if I knew what I was doing. I was two steps ahead of them as we walked in. I asked the lady in the ticket booth which train was ours and she directed us to it. "You'd want to get the legs under ye!" she said in her Limerick City accent.

"Come on, we need to hurry," I said.

We ran to the train and said our goodbyes. We cried,

hugged, kissed and hugged again. Poor ol' Mammy was crying quite a bit. She was very sad seeing two of her five daughters leaving for a year. I kissed and hugged her so, so tight. I turned to Nan and did not want to make a big deal about our goodbye, but she pulled my hand back swiftly as I tried to walk away, and she whispered, "Do you remember what we talked about before you left for England?"

"I do, Nan."

"Well, this is not a practice run. I want you to please stay safe and…"

"Yes, Nan. I know. Listen to my inside voice." I interrupted as she spoke.

"Alicia, you won't always hear my voice, but you will ALWAYS know what I am saying."

"This time it's different, luv. Promise me you will?"

"I promise you, Nana. I promise!" I said as I pushed forward toward the train.

I will never forget the energy and feeling that was generated by our goodbye that day. There was a special embrace and kiss and I felt ready to find my way in a new land.

Tina and I jumped on the train and immediately found a door where we could step out and wave. I was waving and blowing kisses from the train, looking back at Mammy, Nana, Kim and Amy.

That very moment, as we pulled away from the train station, something consumed me. I am not quite sure how to explain it. It was definitely profound and there was zero uncertainty attached to the feeling.

I knew I was not coming home.

I recognized at that moment I could feel and sense something very special. My unnamed emotion held so much conviction, it just could not be wrong. I knew this was part of my destiny--this was where I had to go!

We flew to Iceland and had a seven-and-a-half-hour

layover, and then we flew on to the JFK Airport in New York. We were so excited to get to America and begin the journey we were embarking on.

"Better pass boldly into that other world, in the full glory of some passion, than fade and wither dismally with age."

- James Joyce

Chapter 8

The US of A!

"Get out... I don't want to even look at you. Get out.

Just get out!"

Looking out of the airplane window on the approach to JFK airport, I felt completely in awe.

This is America! Wow, I am here. I made it.

It was almost overwhelming to me. I looked out the window of the plane and could not stop taking in the beauty of New York. It was so much bigger than I had ever imagined. There were endless buildings, huge sky scrapers and millions of cars as far as my eyes could see. Everything was just enormous. The very second I walked off the plane, I took a breath. It was so different. The air itself was different--not only the smells, but the texture, too.

Tina and I had to part ways in JFK. She had a flight to Albany to catch and I was meeting my host Dad, Jack Crowley. Then we were going to drive to Philadelphia from New York. It had been over two days since I'd left Limerick City Train Station and I didn't even feel tired.

I walked out of the security at JFK and there was Mr. Jack Crowley, holding a sign with my name on it. I had never had my name on a sign like that, I felt really special.

Jack had traveled from Philadelphia to New York to pick me up, so we had a long drive back to their house. About halfway there, Jack's phone rang. It was his wife Paula. She was just checking to see if I'd been picked up and that we were on the way back. I remember thinking, *This is going to be great! Phones in cars and everything, just like Dublin!*

When we got to the house, I was like a zombie. I had been traveling about 30+ hours at this stage and I was exhausted. I met Paula and their son David, who was three years old. David was very shy and as cute as a button. William and Caroline were in bed, so I did not get to meet them that night. Paula was absolutely beautiful. She had a demeanor about her that was so warm, kind and inviting.

The next morning, I woke up and I felt like I'd been hit by a truck. I noticed the sunshine and realized it was late morning. I got dressed, walked up the stairs and met the whole family. Caroline had been adopted from Chile and she was six months old. William was only nine weeks old. They were so cute and adorable! Two babies under one year old and I loved that. I had enough kisses and hugs for everyone.

I settled in nicely and we formed a strong bond. I met other nannies and made some fast friends. One of them was named Mary. She was from Ennis in County Clare. County Clare is not that far from Limerick. Mary was just like me. She was a little older, but we were like two peas in a pod.

Paula and Jack were wonderful parents. I felt comfortable and welcomed into their family. I fell in love with the kids. We all had a very special relationship. I would teach them Irish slang words just to be funny.

Paula and Jack converted the downstairs of their house into a bedroom for me. There was a door leading to the outside, so it seemed like it was my own apartment. I loved it so much. I even had a TV in my bedroom. That's a far stretch from the house on the hill or even Mount David!

After a while, I became enthralled with reading American newspapers. Jack would have one delivered each day and I would grab it once he was done with it. This was also my first experience with recycling. Paula and Jack had a recycle bin just for newspapers and a bin just for bottles and cans.

Just for fun, I would pick up a New York Times or a Washington Post on the weekends and try to learn the vocabulary.

It was the second or third month of being there when I first picked up the Washington Post at the shop. I walked home, made a cup of tea, went into the front room and I started reading it right away. I was just fascinated by those two newspapers. I was almost done with the whole thing when I turned to the second-to last-page and there it was--a half-page advertisement for a lottery on green cards. It was for permanent residency to stay in the US. I had to read it about four or five times to make sure I understood it.

There was an actual application for the lottery itself as part of the advertisement. The ad said to include thirty-seven dollar for the application fee. I ripped the ad out of the paper, filled in my information and put thirty-seven dollars in cash in an envelope. I put the envelope on my desk and actually forgot about it for about a week. I came across it after cleaning my room and I went upstairs and asked Paula if she had a stamp. She gave me a stamp and I stuck it on the envelope. I hadn't written a return address on the envelope and it had a twenty-dollar bill, a ten-dollar bill, a five-dollar bill and two one-dollar bills inside.

That is a fact!

I put the envelope in the mailbox for the mail carrier to pick up when he dropped off the mail the next day. About three months later, Paula called me up to the kitchen because I'd received a letter in the mail from the Department of Immigration/Naturalization. I assumed it was from the agency about my trip home, even though it said US Immigration on the envelope. I opened it and tried to read it, but I could not comprehend it. Paula was standing beside me, asking me what it was about.

I handed her the letter and said, "I dunno. Can you tell me?"

She started reading, glanced up at me and then back down at the letter, and again back at me. She asked, "Alicia, did you apply for anything to get a Visa?"

"No, I didn't," I said, puzzled. She sat down and began to read more carefully. Suddenly, she stood up, grabbed me by the arm and started screaming...

"It says you won a lottery for a permanent green card and that you have to go back to Ireland to the American Consulate for an interview!"

Then it all came back to me...

"Oh--now I remember! I filled out this thing in the paper and sent thirty-seven dollars with it," I said.

"You sent cash to a lottery for green cards to Washington DC?" She asked, clearly surprised.

"I did, yeah. Was I not supposed to?" I asked.

After looking into it more, Paula found out that there were millions of applicants for this lottery. She brought home information about it. People had hired lawyers to apply thousands of times by the deadline, but for some reason, my torn-out application with cash made it all the way and was actually picked. It was truly a lot to digest.

Now my focus in the next few weeks was on what I was supposed to do and how I was supposed to do it. Paula and Jack offered to pay for my ticket back home to Ireland to go through whatever process I needed to, in order to return to the states and stay on as their nanny. I felt truly blessed. They didn't have to do that.

I was notified via letter when my appointment was in Dublin. Paula bought the plane ticket for me and off I went. I think back now on how selfless Paula really was. She was just an amazing person inside and out. Paula drove me to the airport and I jumped on the plane home to the Ol' Emerald Isle, The Motherland!

I had to fly into Dublin and do a slew of interviews and see the certified doctor who was named in my letter from the American Consulate. I didn't have anyone meet me in the airport as I was only in Ireland for a few days. I was required to be examined by a specific doctor in Dublin and get blood drawn at the hospital and then go to the American Consulate to be interviewed.

I didn't have a lot of money, so Mammy asked my Uncle Dennis and Aunt Peg if I could stay with them in Dublin while I got everything sorted. I got all of my appointments checked off my list and then it was time for the actual interview at the American Consulate. The officer asked me a bunch of questions and asked what my intention in the US was. My intention....? What a fecken silly question, my intention. Can you just imagine if I'd said I intended to break the law and not be an upstanding person. Fecken eegit! Jesus, it was hectic. I felt like I pretty much signed away my firstborn to the US Immigration/Naturalization Service.

Finally, it was all done and over with. I could not believe it. I'd just been issued a green card for America, the US of A!

I knew this was my destiny. It was that feeling I'd had at the Limerick City Train Station which finally came to fruition. It was that very thought the day I waved goodbye to Nana, Mammy, Kim and Amy.

I headed back to the US to start my new life. After I got back to the Crowley's, Paula and Jack introduced me to this girl called Marti. She was a nanny for friends of theirs who lived about two miles away.

Marti was a home-grown girl from Nebraska. She and I hit it off straight away. She was a big girl with shoulder-length wavy hair and a full set of brilliant white teeth. She was very pretty and we soon became good friends. The nice thing about it was, Marti had a car. We could drive around the place as teenagers like they did in the movies. She would come pick me up after work and we would go to Dairy Queen for ice cream a couple of times a week. She called me every day and we saw each other probably three to four times a week. She would show me around the area and introduce me to friends of hers. I felt like I'd met a good friend.

One weekend in August, the family Marti worked for was going out of town for the weekend and Marti wanted to invite some friends over. She knew some boys that were in the Navy and were stationed in Philly. She asked them if they wanted to come to the party. I was excited to meet American boys. The whole thing reminded me of one of my favourite movies, **Say Anything** with John Cusack, that was, and still is, one of my favourite movies of all time (second only to **The Color Purple**.)

That afternoon, I found myself really looking forward to my first teenage American party. So Marti and I went to the mall and bought some new outfits for that night. I have a picture of me in that atrocious get-up somewhere, but it was not one of my most memorable looks. I bought black leggings with white polka dots and a crop top in white with black polka dots. It was definitely a crime against fashion, but back then I felt like I was the bomb-digidty!

After we got back from the mall, we went to the grocery store called Acme to buy some chips and dip and other American party stuff. Marty was twenty-one, so she could pick up beer and wine, too. We went to Marty's house to shower and get ready. I remember getting out of the shower and feeling like I was already sweating with the humidity and heat. We put **Ace of Base** on her stereo and cranked it up to ten while we blow-dried our hair and put on a bit of makeup to make us feel pretty. I wore lipstick that day, which I rarely did. It was so much fun, and very different from Foynes and Shanagolden.

The house was amazing. It reminded me of the house in **Risky Business** with Tom Cruise in his tighty-whities dancing across the floor with a broom in his hands. It was a giant house-- probably about five or six times bigger than #8 Woodvale, for sure. It was nestled into a wooded area and it had a huge driveway with a roundabout in the middle of it. There were three windows on each side of the front door and six windows on the second floor. It was white and had black shutters on every single window.

Marti and I set everything up in the screened-in backyard porch. There was a little pond surrounded by dense trees and woods so there were bugs everywhere.

That was the night I met him--Sean Flatley.

There was a definite spark between us and we started seeing each other. I knew I had strong feelings for Sean and I was so happy I did not have to leave in April after my year was up on the *Au Pair* contract.

I knew this was all in my destiny, my fate, my path.

I felt so drawn to him and his charismatic personality. He would pull the chair out for me before I sat down and would ask me if I needed anything or refill on my drink if it was empty. He was dreamy, with mysterious dark eyes, gelled, groomed hair and a lovely smile. His teeth were so white and straight. I wasn't used to seeing such white straight teeth in Ireland. It was more like a dull, off-white, almost yellow teeth, with at least one if not two obvious gaps as the norm.

We felt like we belonged together, well at least, I did. I was very content just being with him. I did not want to go out with anyone else. Sean just seemed right to me.

Sean would drive up to Stratford from Philadelphia to see me. It was about a twenty-five minute drive so he would come a few times a week. Paula and Jack welcomed him into their home and even allowed him to stay over with me in the lower level on weekends.

It was February in Philadelphia and it was cold. I remember feeling the cartilage in my ears hurting so much from the humid cold. I was very excited to spend my first Valentine's day with Sean. I was eager to see what he would get me. Would it be flowers, chocolate or even a teddy bear? Maybe one of those huge cards and balloons?

I heard his car pull up outside the house and I ran over to the window to take a peek at what he'd got me. He got out of the car, opened the back boot and pulled out a huge bunch of balloons with ribbons. And then I also saw him grab a box. I remember the feeling I got from realizing he'd gone to that effort for me. I ran back downstairs to my room and pretended like I hadn't seen him pull out the balloons. He walked in the door and I acted so surprised, I ran over to him with my arms open and gave him a big hug and kiss. I'd got him a card and I wrote a poem for him inside. I gave him the card and we kissed and hugged. It was a great experience. I will always remember that Valentine's day. I was so in love with him and thought I was such a lucky girl.

Paula and Jack were going out for dinner that evening and they had asked me to babysit for them. I said of course I would. I didn't mind at all--but Sean did, I guess. He was pretty upset that I had agreed to babysit on Valentine's day evening.

I told him that I would cook something for us and we could have a nice dinner after I put the kids to bed. He was not thrilled about it, so that kinda put a damper on the evening. This was one of the first times I saw that side of him. It was more adolescent behaviour than adult behavior. He pouted and wouldn't answer my questions. I felt like I had ruined our evening.

I put the kids to bed and went downstairs to tell Sean I was starting dinner. He was asleep in my bed, so I left him there and started preparing the food. I had found a recipe in the Readers Digest and had kept it especially for this special dinner. It was lemon chicken with walnuts and watercress. I'd bought everything I needed to make an amazing meal. I had Paula buy me some wine for it, too.

Another few months into our relationship, I found out Sean was cheating on me. He was seeing another girl at the base. Her father was an officer in the Navy, so they were able to hang out on the base together. As for me, I would need to get signed in and out of the base.

I was devastated. Why would he do that to me? I just didn't understand it. Marti had been the one to tell me he was hanging out with another girl.

I didn't know what I should do. Nobody had ever chosen to be with someone else when they'd been with me (other than Botty, but that wasn't the same.) I did not know what to do. I felt a fire in my belly. It was a powerful sense of dread, and I couldn't sleep or eat.

This was probably one of the first times I recognized that my body has an immediate physical reaction to anything that upsets me.

I decided to confront him about it. He denied it at first, but I told him that one of his friends had told Marti and then she'd told me. I told him that we could ask Marti together, and that's when he confessed. He begged me to give him a second chance and he promised it would never happen again. He sat on the edge of the couch with his hands clenched between his open knees. He hung

his head in shame and his voice was shaky and sad. He looked up

at me with tears in his eyes and said, "Please, please forgive me,

Alicia. I really fucked up and I don't deserve you. You deserve so

much better than me. I will do anything to prove I am meant to be

with you. Anything. Just let me know and I will do it. Please

forgive me!"

"Sean, it's not that easy to do. You betrayed me, my trust,

my love. I'm not sure if I can."

"Will you try, Alicia? Will you, please? I will try 100%, I

promise you."

"Okay, I will try. That's all I can do for now," I replied

reluctantly.

Sean was so considerate after that day I was sure things

were going to be much different going forward. He would bring

me flowers for no reason at all, bring me out to dinner on a

Wednesday night and he even wrote me a poem and read it to me. I

felt like we were going to be okay.

Sean would stay over with me almost every weekend and we began to repair our relationship.

Paula and Jack bought a larger house in St. David's, PA. It was only about four miles from the old house. I had the top floor of the new house. It was really nice. It was a Victorian-style three-story mansion. It had a round room that looked like it was a church. It had stained glass arched windows all the way around the room and a huge fireplace as a focal point. It was just magnificent.

Sometimes, Paula and Jack would take the kids to the Jersey Shore to Paula's parents for the weekend. On this particular weekend, it was my birthday. Mammy had sent me a birthday card with a hundred-dollar bill inside as a gift for me to go buy myself something nice. Sean and I had planned on going out to dinner to celebrate. I was so excited for our date I had even bought a new outfit to wear. I asked Sean to think about where we should go and I went to take a shower.

After I got out of the shower, I went into my room. Sean was gone. I looked out the window and his car was gone. I figured he must have run out to the store for something. I finished getting ready and then just sat there waiting and waiting and waiting.

After two hours, I was getting really worried and thought maybe something had happened to him. But, then I thought, if something had happened, why didn't he tell me before he left?

I was baffled. We had plans for dinner for my birthday. Where the feck did he go? Hour after hour passed. I stayed up all night with my stomach in knots. I just laid on my bed hugging a pillow. The sun was starting to come up when I heard his car pull in. He walked into my room still wearing the sweats he used as pajamas, which was weird.

"Oh my God Sean, what happened? Where were you? I have been up all night. I didn't know what happened. Are you all right?" I asked.

"I'm fine. Nothing's wrong. I did something horrible and I don't know if you will forgive me," he said.

Immediately I thought he'd cheated on me again.

"What did you do?" I asked.

He looked at me and said, "I took your hundred-dollar bill

out of the birthday card your mother sent you and spent it."

"WHAT are you talking about? Why would you do that? What did you spend it on?" I yelled.

Sean stood right in front of me, looked down to the ground and said, "I spent it on cocaine."

"Oh my God! What is wrong with you? You do drugs? I can't believe what I am hearing! I thought you ran out to the shop and got in an accident or something. Get out. I don't want to even look at you. Get out. Just get out!" I screamed.

I thought I was dreaming. This seemed unreal!

Sean wouldn't leave. He started crying and saying, "I don't know why I did it. I am so sorry! Please forgive me. I will never do this again, I promise."

He groveled, he cried and he begged. I just could not comprehend that someone would not only take my birthday money but leave me knowing I didn't know where he went.

And to buy drugs? Who does that? Jesus Christ Almighty.

This was like I was in a movie or something. It took me

quite a while to digest what had happened. I didn't know how to process all of this. I asked him to leave me alone and not contact me anymore. He would not leave. He wore me down with his pathetic words and I ended up shoving it under the carpet and hoping we could get over this incident and grow to trust each other again.

"Why is it we don't heed the heart, when we know for a fact what it is telling us?"

~ Alicia McMahon

Chapter 9

My Beautiful Buggie

"I don't think you understand the severity of this

situation, Mrs. Flatley. This could be life-threatening."

A few months later I discovered I was pregnant. Nineteen years old and pregnant. Wow! What would I do now?

I sat on this information for a while and digested it for myself. Should I tell Mammy before I told Sean? Should I tell Paula and get her advice on how to handle this? What should I do? I still had to watch David, Caroline and Will, and it was hard to continue to work while I felt shitty with morning sickness.

That's it. I decided that I was going to tell Sean when he came over next. I was very nervous about it. I didn't know how he would feel. What if he left me and then I would be left all alone in this foreign country with a baby?

Later that evening, Sean came up to St. David's to see me. I was lying down in bed, just feeling like crap. He walked into the room and said, "What's wrong with you? Are you sick?"

I looked over at him and said, "You might want to sit down for this."

"You are pregnant, aren't you?" he asked immediately.

"Yes, I'm pregnant, Sean," I replied, and I waited to see the expression on his face.

He immediately started to smile and he hugged me. Right then, I felt great. I was not going to be alone. I would be okay. We would be okay.

Holy Shit... I'm going to have a baby! I kept saying that over and over again in my head.

That night was just lovely. Sean held me and hugged me and made me feel safe.

We talked about what we were going to do. I decided to make a phone call to Mammy and tell her the next day. Sean said he would wait to tell his parents until next week after I spoke to mine.

The next morning, I got up and went downstairs to make some tea and toast for breakfast and then called my Mam. I was pretty straightforward on the phone and got straight to the point after our, "How are you," and, "How's the weather?"

"Mammy, I'm pregnant."

… Crickets… Silence…Nothing…

Then I said, "Mam? Are you there Mammy?"

She replied with, "How do you feel about it, Alicia?"

"I'm happy, Mammy, and so is Sean," I said.

"What are you going to do?"

"We are going to have the baby and probably get married," I replied.

"Well, okay luv, if that's what you want, then we are

behind you," she said.

I knew she was taken aback and was not as excited about it as I was. But I suppose, what could she do? I knew by the tone of her voice I was disappointing her, and that hurt to hear.

Sean and I got married in Ireland on December 23rd, 1992. Sean's parents, Bill and Anna, and brother Mike came to Ireland for the wedding. Sean wore full formal Navy garb and I got married in the quintessential wedding dress--you know, with the puffy shoulders and sequins in the front. We were married in Foynes Village Church for all the villagers to see.

After we got married, I had to move out to Colorado to Sean's parents' house because he was going out to sea for a few months with the Navy and then would be docking in San Diego. Then the plan was that he would come to Colorado and move the baby and me out to San Diego until he got discharged. I said my goodbyes to Paula, Jack, David, Caroline and Will and flew out to Colorado, where Sean's parents picked me up.

It was definitely an adjustment for me to move into his

parents' house and not see him for months. The plan was, he would call me at each port, send me his wages and I would save it so we could get a place in San Diego. But unfortunately, he would get to port and blow through all his wages.

On one occasion I got a call from him when he was in St. Thomas. He said he was mugged and they'd taken his shoes and he had to buy more. Another time he said he lost his wallet. So, I don't think I got one month of wages from him total. It seemed like there was an excuse--every single month. I ended up having to find a job just so I had enough money to survive. Anna's sister Reba was an Allstate agent and she hired me part-time to work as a receptionist. I was very grateful to her for doing that for me.

There I was, pregnant, living with his parents, alone and scared. I really missed home. I longed for my parents and sisters. It was a rough time for me emotionally. I felt abandoned and alone most of the time. I wanted to be with my family so desperately. I wanted to have my Mammy with me to answer the questions I had during pregnancy. I wanted my sisters' support and hugs and I wanted to share in my excitement with them. I missed my Nana. I kept going over a conversation I'd had with Nana just after I got married. I remember she said, "You are making your own life now, luv. Don't forget who you are. Don't let any man put his hands on you. Always listen to your gut, it will never do you wrong. I promise."

The time was getting close to having my baby and I found out it was a girl… a girl…Oh, Janey Mackers! A baby girl! ☺

My baby was due on June 23rd. It was now July 1st and I was miserable. I was still living in Anna and Bill's house and Sean was still at sea. Being July in Colorado, the temperature was over a hundred degrees and I was walking around like a baby elephant. I'd had my bags packed and ready by the front door since June 1st and I'd had a couple of times where I' thought it was time, but they were good ol' Braxton Hicks.

On July 2nd, I went to bed, leaving Anna and Bill in the kitchen drinking, as they did a few times a week. I wasn't feeling very good that night. At about 1:00 am I woke up with excruciating back pain. I had to get up and get some water. It took me about two minutes to get out of the bed. I opened the door and walked out into the hallway and I had to hold on to the wall because the pain was so intense. I knew something was up. I did not have contractions, just back pain.

I got my water and headed back to bed. I went to go lay down and tried to go back to sleep, but the back spasms just kept getting worse and worse. I could only put up with it another hour or so and then I decided to wake up Anna and Bill. We called the hospital and they said to come in. Anna and Bill were hustling to leave, and I just sat on the chair with my hospital bag, waiting.

The smell of mouthwash was very strong. I guess after having a few drinks they were trying to hide the smell of alcohol. On the way to the hospital I could not stop looking at the full moon and trying to manage the pain in my back.

The military hospital was at Lowery Air Force Base about thirty-five minutes away. That seemed like hours to me. Once we got there they admitted me and said I was 3 ½ centimeters dilated. It was about 6:00 am and they broke my water, gave me an epidural and said it would help the progression.

Now it was around noon and I was having major spasms in my back. I started shaking and feeling cold. They tried to put a monitor on my baby's head, which was a needle that they stuck on the baby's scalp while she was still inside me. This was a teaching hospital, so this medical student had to try a few times. They'd noticed my baby was stressing and they just wanted to monitor us.

The pain actually started to get worse for me. I was over twelve hours in hard labor and I was exhausted. I could not believe being in labor was this hard. After another few hours they figured out I was getting an infection in my womb, because my water had been broken for hours and I was just 6 cm dilated.

Now my baby was in serious distress and alarms started going off. I was so scared. The doctor came in and said they were going to have to do an emergency C-Section because the baby's heart rate was progressively getting weaker and after eighteen hours in labor, I was still only 6 ½ cm dilated.

Within ten minutes, I was lying down in surgery. There were about six people in the room and I was really frightened and awake! The surgeon started to make an incision and I screamed "I'm going to throw up!"

He replied, "Ma'am, do you feel that?"

"Yes, I do. It really hurts!" I shouted.

"Get anesthesiology in here now," He ordered the nurse.

I guess the epidural had worn off after twelve hours, but they'd thought I was numb. I had to lay there for about ten more minutes until I was given another epidural, but the incision was open the entire time. The next thing I heard was the surgeon saying, "We are going to have to get this baby out now!"

I will never forget that feeling when they were pulling my baby out of me. I could feel everything, even hands inside my womb. I just wanted my baby to be okay. I felt a lot of pressure and then all of a sudden, this huge relief when I heard the nurse say, "Congratulations, Mrs. Flatley. It's a girl!"

I started uncontrollably crying with joy and relief when I heard her cry. Welcome

Séanalee Alta, 6 lbs., 3 oz. and 18 inches long. They took her, wiped her down and let me kiss her just before they walked her out of the room.

I felt like I needed to throw up and asked the nurse if she could grab a bowl. I threw up yellow bile or some type of mucus. It was horrible. They stapled me up and wheeled me out of the surgery room.

I kept asking when I could see my baby and they kept saying, "Soon." They took me up to my room and said they would check on my daughter. After the longest ten minutes of my life. A nurse came in and said my baby was in intensive care. She had a heart murmur and they wanted to monitor it. I immediately asked,

"Can I go to her? I need to see her. I am breastfeeding."

The nurse replied, "We are still doing some tests on her. I will let you know as soon as we are done."

The anxiety and sheer desperation I felt of not being able to see, hold, touch or kiss my child was indescribable. I felt total panic. Didn't they understand? I wanted to see my baby!

I must have fallen asleep, because when I woke up it was dark. I opened my eyes and looked around the room for Séanalee, but I was alone. I called for a nurse and someone came into the room.

"I need to see my baby now!" I told the nurse sternly.

"Okay. Let me check and I will be right back," she stated.

After about five minutes she returned with a wheelchair and said, "Are you ready to meet your baby, Mrs. Flatley?"

"Thank you so much," I said, and started crying at the same time.

I'd forgotten about my surgery and started to get out of the bed and I felt the sharpest pain ever and fell to the ground. I didn't care, though. I was going to meet my baby! The nurse was a bit panicked that I had collapsed and fell to the floor, but I told her I was fine. She wheeled me two floors up to intensive care and there was my baby, Séanalee. They lifted her out of the little incubator and put her in my arms.

My whole body flooded with intense happiness and joy. I felt overwhelmed and overcome with a feeling I'd never experienced before. Is this what motherhood felt like? I stroked her soft, buttery cheek, kissed her and smelled her neck. I felt like I could burst with joy and love for her. The experience was so intense and natural I loved feeling like that.

She was so angelic, just beautiful, a perfect little face and reddish blonde hair!

I'd made her inside me. She was mine! All mine!!!

I noticed there was a round scab on her head and I ask what it was from. They said it was from the monitor they tried to insert during labor. It was a little hole in her head. I felt so bad for her, but I knew she was mine. They explained to me that she had a hole in her heart and they wanted to keep her in intensive care for a little while.

I asked them if I could feed her and the doctor said yes, but they'd had to give her a bottle earlier because she was hungry. I was so upset about that. I did not want my baby to have formula and I wanted to nurse her myself. I tried to breastfeed her there in the wheelchair, but it was not working. I was positive it was because they'd given her a bottle earlier. I started crying again. I felt like they'd robbed me of the first couple of hours of my infant's life.

I tried to nurse her for about forty-five minutes and then one of the nurses said that they needed to put her back into the incubator. I was taken back down to my room and put into bed. The Flatley's were already down there when I returned. They said they'd called my parents and let them know and they'd called the Navy to notify Sean. I had one of those morphine drips for pain and the nurse had hit the button, so by now I was starting to feel groggy.

I was really having a hard time breathing. My lungs felt so restricted and I couldn't take a deep breath. All of a sudden an alarm went off and two nurses ran into the room. They also called the doctor, who showed up about twenty minutes later in his pajamas. They did a few tests and then told me that I had a pulmonary embolism. There was a blood clot about ½ an inch from entering my left lung.

The doctor said, "We should operate as soon as possible."

All I kept thinking was I would not get to see my baby that

night. I said, "No. No more operations!"

The doctor replied, "I don't think you understand the severity of this situation, Mrs. Flatley. This could be life threatening."

Anna jumped right in and said, "Alicia, you don't know what you are saying. You just had morphine. Please listen to the doctor."

Then she asked, "Doctor, can I decide for her?"

"Unfortunately, no. It needs to be either her husband or a parent/guardian," he said.

Right then, Anna and Bill tried to call back the military and locate Sean at sea. He was somewhere in South America. After Anna called, the Navy put a helicopter on standby in case this got any worse. They were unable to make direct contact with Sean, so they called my mother in Ireland.

The doctor, still in his PJ's, was on the phone explaining to my mother how serious this was. The doctor passed the phone to Anna and she explained to Mammy that if the clot moved ½ an inch into my lung they might not have much time to save me. It was obvious by Anna's reaction that Mammy had asked to speak to me.

"Alicia, darling, are you okay?" she asked, desperation in her voice.

"I'm okay, Mammy. I am not going back in for more surgery. I only saw Séanalee once and they already gave her a bottle without asking me. I want to feed her at 11:30, dammit," I said.

"Alicia are you 100% sure, luv?" she asked. "This is very serious, and we want you to be here to raise your daughter."

"Mammy, I'm sure!" I replied.

"Okay, Luv, pass me back to the doctor. I love you darling and I will call you tomorrow."

I can't even imagine being my mother in Ireland with her daughter in a life-threatening situation in America and not being able to be with her.

I passed the phone back to the doctor and she told him, no surgery. He seemed a little agitated and concerned when he got off the phone. He ordered the nurse to get a blood thinner in the IV drip, stat.

Now I was in intensive care, too! This sucked! I didn't care how I was feeling. I insisted they wheel me up to Séanalee for every feeding to try and nurse her. She just wasn't latching on. I felt so inadequate and I didn't understand why.

After the third day, the head nurse came into my room and said, "You are determined to breastfeed your baby Mrs. Flatley. You are on separate floors and are both in intensive care. I think it's ridiculous, I am ordering them to bring her down here, so we can monitor her from your room."

I was so relieved and happy. Séanalee was at my bedside about an hour later and I picked her up, closed the curtain around my bed and tried to nurse her. She nursed right away.

Yes, success! I can't tell you how relieved and happy I was.

We were both taken out of intensive care the next day and we spent a total of about two weeks in the hospital. I needed blood thinners the entire time for the pulmonary embolism.

After we returned to Anna and Bill's house, we both started

healing and feeling better. It was quite a challenge trying to be a new Mammy with Anna there. She was very insistent on some things. She would force me to do things her way when it came to caring for my baby. I would put Séanalee down for a nap on her tummy and Anna would blatantly walk in and put her on her back--ya know, things like that.

Sean came to Colorado when Séanalee was about five weeks old. I couldn't wait to see him. I couldn't wait for him to see our beautiful little child.

He was only in Colorado for two weeks, so right after we had the Christening we packed up the car and headed on our road trip to San Diego. On to our new life. Sean's brother Mike already lived there so he drove back with us after the Christening.

The plan was to make it in two days. Sean had a place lined up for us in La Mesa, just outside of San Diego. We were sharing a house with his aunt and cousin. They were renting rooms in the lower floor of this house and there was another room available.

We drove straight to Las Vegas and got a hotel room. I had

managed to save $225.00 from working part-time during my pregnancy.

It was late by the time we got to Las Vegas. We got something to eat and went to the room. As soon as we got there, I took a shower and then bathed Séanalee. Sean was just itching to go gamble and I was a little upset, because we had no money for food, let alone gambling. I went to bed with my baby and they went out. A couple of hours later I heard someone in the room and I was startled. The lights were off, but there was someone there.

I sat up and said, "Sean, is that you?"

"Yeah, it's me. Go back to sleep," he replied.

"What are you doing?" I asked.

"Nothing. I said go back to sleep," he said sternly.

Then I realized what he was doing. He was in my purse, taking our money. I knew he was going to go and gamble it away. That's all we had until he got paid in two days. I got out of bed and told him he couldn't take it, but he did anyway.

Why would he do that? There we were, driving into San Diego the next morning with a six-week-old baby trying to start a new life with no money. This was horrible. We were flat fecken broke!

This behavior carried on and on. I never had money. I always had to fight for nappies and formula. I nursed her as long as I could. I never had cash in my pocket. It was so hard to keep everything going.

We had rented a room in a house where Sean's Aunt Sharon also lived. We had one room each and we shared the living room and kitchen. I was a little relieved to know that we would be with family and we would not be completely alone.

However, this feeling did not last too long. It was pretty nice for the first couple of weeks. Sean would go to work and come home each night at the same time. I had a glimpse of normal family life.

I used to make banana nut muffins and we would have them each night while watching Jeopardy at 6:30 pm. I would prop Séanalee up in her bouncy chair in the middle of us and we would all watch it together.

We only had one car, so whenever I had any appointments for the baby I would have to drive Sean to the Coronado Navy base. It was nerve-wracking at first. I would be driving down a six-lane highway with the little peanut in the back in her car seat and people from California drove like mad. Everyone was in a hurry and everyone was impatient.

Sean's Aunt Sharon did not have a car, so on the days I would have it she would always ask to use it. It got to the point where I would be waiting for her to return our car so I could go pick up Sean after work. There were many times I was out on the stoop with Séanalee in her car seat all buckled up and ready to go, just waiting for Sharon to bring back the car. It was such a struggle living there. I really didn't like living in San Diego. It didn't feel right to me.

Finally, the day came that we were moving back to Colorado. Sean was actually honourably discharged. I was so happy. Maybe we could be normal now, like a real family.

"There is a dissimilar, horrible pain that comes with loving someone more than they love you." ~ Alicia McMahon

Chapter 10

My Darling Dowser

I remember asking myself how I got to this point.

How could I fix this? How could I fix him?

We drove back to Colorado when Séanalee was about five

months old. We rented a townhouse a couple of miles from Sean's

parents' house and that is where I saw the real man I had married.

I did not know this, but I found out the reason Sean had

enlisted in the Navy was to get away from drug use in Colorado. It did not take long for all his old habits to return. Sean became someone I did not know. I didn't know how to react to his behaviours, his lies and his self-centeredness. I realized there was no changing what I knew deep in my soul. I had married an abusive, drug-addicted, alcoholic gambler and compulsive liar.

And to make matters worse, I found out I was pregnant again. I think I had blinders on, pretending I could fix our marriage and make him better, but I could not deny reality any longer.

He would go over to his sister's house and do crack, pot and cocaine. I felt like I was in a movie sometimes. Why didn't anyone understand this was not okay? His sister would just let him do drugs at her house. It was just surreal!

It got really bad during my second pregnancy. I think Sean was doing so much crack he would hallucinate and get extremely paranoid. He wouldn't sleep. He'd stay up all night and go to work strung out. I knew in my heart this was crazy behavior. It's hard to explain how I felt about the way he was acting at the time. Looking back on it now, I knew he was out of control. I should have paid attention to my intuition.

A few months later, my cousin Coco came to visit me for a few days. It was a lot different from our shenanigans in Ireland and France, but it was a blessing to see her. It was during her visit that Sean first punched me with his fists. He usually hit me with his open hand or pushed me, up until this night. It felt so warped and surreal. It is hard to describe even in my head.

He wanted me to go get something. I can't remember what it was, but I was in bed and didn't want to get up because I was seven months pregnant. He pushed his face directly onto my cheek and said with his teeth clenched together, "Get the fuck up, you lazy bitch!"

He ended up pushing me out of the bed with his feet. I know Coco heard me fall on the floor from my bed. It was impossible not to.

Once on the floor, I took a second to make sure I was okay.

I went into the fetal position and protected my baby. He came down to the floor and with closed fists started punching me. I was in the fetal position crying and trying to hold in the sounds of my crying because I didn't want Coco to hear me. I felt so embarrassed and ashamed.

I heard my Nana Murphy's voice at that very moment. "This is not okay!" "What is wrong with you? This needs to stop, Alicia!"

I chose not to act on anything right then, but I heard her. It was not what I expected. It was my voice with Nana's sternness, yet is was familiar to me.

I saw clarity that night. I was living in a warped reality. This was damaging my child, and in a few weeks, I was to have my new baby. I was all my little girl would have to rely on. I knew that now, but I had no idea what was coming my way.

After Coco left, I mustered up the courage and told Anna and Bill what had happened. They said that he was just under a lot of pressure and it would be better soon. It was like they just dismissed it. I thought they would stand up for me and Séanalee, but I guess not.

That weekend, we brought Séanalee over and we had dinner at Anna and Bill's house. It got a little heated between Bill and Sean. Sean was just irrational 24/7. Sean, Anna and Bill were all drinking before dinner and then continued to drink after dinner. They were all pretty drunk by 9:30 pm and I just wanted to lay down with Séanalee and go to sleep.

They were getting pretty buzzed when Anna asked Sean if he ever hit me. He immediately glared at me with anger in his eyes and said, "Of course I don't! I would never hit my wife, never mind my pregnant wife."

Why would she ask him like that, and especially with me there? It was as if she was asking about the weather.

I knew this was just going to be pushed under the rug and I wanted to actually say something about it. I knew I had to--I had heard my Crone voice!

I stood right up and said," Yes you did! And if that ever

happens again, I will not have my children around a man who hits his wife".

Anna turned her head and looked at me with disgust in her eyes. She was so angry with me and I don't know why. She started yelling at me saying, "They are not just *YOUR* children, they are *MY* grandchildren! Séanalee is mine. You can never take her away from us!"

This was sounding crazy. I think I looked at this family as being nuts. Really! It began to be more and more obvious to me that I could not talk to Anna or Sean's sister Nora about anything to do with Sean. They were his best cheering squad and made me feel inadequate for even questioning his behavior. This became a lonely and scary time for me. I was doubting myself and losing my confidence. I felt so alone.

Over the next few weeks, things didn't get better. As a matter of fact, they were getting worse. He just stopped coming home after work and when he finally did come home, it was four or five in the morning and he would have to be at work by 7:30 am. I honestly do not know how he could do that. I would ask him,

"Why aren't you coming home?" and he would do as he always did, make me feel bad and start an argument. I was getting worn down. I was coming up on my due date and I started the nesting stage--washing everything, dusting and scrubbing the kitchen and dining room floor on my hands and knees. I vacuumed everywhere, even the corners of the stairs. All I needed was some money to buy groceries. This was all part of the preparation for my new baby. I could not wait to hold her in my arms and kiss her. I longed to see my new daughter.

The day was December 13th, 1995. I had to be at the hospital by noon. I had everything set up at home and ready for us. I had asked Sean to go to the shop and pick up some chips, dip, snacks and maybe some soda and beers for visitors when they came to see the new baby.

We got to the hospital and I was already 3 cm dilated. The doctor came in and put me on a drip with the inducing drug oxytocin in it. After about two hours, I started feeling pressure.

Sean had fallen asleep and I really did not want him to wake up.

I waited until about 4:30 pm and hit the button for the nurse. The nurse came in, checked me and said I was 8 cm dilated. So they broke my water just after 5:30 pm and the contractions were more consistent. I was so excited to experience a normal childbirth. By now I had the overwhelming urge to push. I literally pushed eight times and my beautiful daughter had arrived.

Brennalynn Miriam was 7 lbs. 1 oz. and 19 inches long and was born at 6:01 pm. She was beautiful. She had sallow skin, big sapphire blue eyes like my sister Jenny and the prettiest face I had ever seen. Bill and Anna came with little Séanalee and we introduced her to her baby sister. She was so excited. I could tell by the look in her eyes and the shine on her face. Even though she was only 2 ½, she was a proud big sister.

After the visit, Bill and Anna said that they were taking Séanalee with them to their house for the night. I actually did not question it at the time. It made perfect sense, given Sean's drugged up state that no one would admit to or say out loud.

That evening, everyone had left by 9:00 pm and I was able to just take a breath and nurse my beautiful child. She was so easy in comparison to her older sister. Brennalynn was a very solemn infant. Her demeanor was so different than Séanalee's as a baby. She was mellow and easygoing, and I was able to nurse her right away! Both of us had a wonderful night, bonding and loving each other. She woke a couple of times to nurse and then she went right back to sleep.

The next morning, the doctor came into my room early. He gave me a once-over and said, "Okay, Mrs. Flatley, you can go home today."

I could not believe it. It was literally twelve hours ago I had given birth, not even a full day! I was very excited, and I called Sean to come pick us up. I got all of our stuff together and we waited for about two hours. He hadn't showed up after three, so I called him again. He eventually showed up, and the second he walked through my hospital room door I could tell he was high on something.

I took one look at him and I started yelling, "You can't drive us like that. You've taken drugs!"

He was getting nervous because I was raising my voice saying the word *drugs*. I started crying. I couldn't believe he was standing in front of me high on crack or something. I couldn't even reason with him.

I said, "Give me the car keys. I am driving us home."

Surprisingly, he agreed. I think it's only because I was so upset. I put my hand out and he reluctantly dropped them in my hand. He was staring at me as if he was disgusted. I put Brennalynn into the car seat and carried her and my bags to the car. I strapped her in and closed the door. Then I got into the car and drove us home. I opened the front door of the townhouse and immediately noticed a horrible stale smell and realized all my candles were burned completely to the end.

"What happened here, Sean? What is that horrible smell?" I yelled at him.

Sean told me he had stayed up all night doing drugs with a friend. I could not describe the fire I felt in my stomach. It was almost like this whole situation was in a movie and I was watching it from outside looking in.

I brought Brennalynn into the house and fed her, changed her, put her in the bassinette and made sure she was asleep. I opened up the windows, trying to air out the house for my newborn baby. Then I went to the store to pick up crackers and snacks and milk.

I got into the car and started crying uncontrollably, just sobbing. I wiped my face and drove to the shop. As I was pushing the cart, my stomach muscles started really hurting me and the pressure on my cervix was almost unbearable. I felt some blood running down my legs and I rushed to the bathroom to wet some paper towels and clean myself up.

I started crying again and could not stop. I just had to get it done and get back to my infant as soon as possible. I started feeling guilty about leaving her asleep and in his care. I got home and carried in the bags from the car. I was exhausted. I put the bags in the kitchen and went up to check my child and there Sean was, passed out on the bed by the bassinette.

I carried the bassinette downstairs so I could watch her while I put everything away and tidied up the house after his partying. I barely got the groceries put away when Anna and Bill came over with Séanalee. Then a whole bunch of Sean's aunts and uncles came and before I knew it, the house was full.

Sean, who had woken up, was playing the proud father role to everyone who came over. I looked at him and watched how he interacted with everyone and thought to myself – *God, you are such a faker, liar, thief and a disgrace! How did I end up with my family being like this? I remember asking myself how I got to this point. How could I fix this? How could I fix him?*

I never mentioned anything about Sean staying up all night doing drugs to anyone. I think I was just too embarrassed and mortified. I felt wronged during this amazing time. I felt such sadness for my beautiful girls. All I wanted was to get Séanalee and Brennalynn away from this poisoned and warped sense of reality.

I would look forward to him leaving for work and then I

could start our day without him. If I was lucky, he would go to his

sister's house and do that shit over there. There are times when I

don't think he actually slept. Just showered and went back out to

work. You know, thinking back at it now, I really think the human

psyche has a way of protecting and almost camouflaging oneself

from hurt and reality. I mustered up what courage I had left and

protected my girls. They were my number one priority.

After a few weeks, my Mammy and Daddy came to visit. I

was so happy, so giddy inside. Now I would get to see my parents

while they spent time with their granddaughters. Now I wouldn't

have to worry about anything. Mammy and Daddy were here!

Séanalee and I had visited Ireland when she was just a year

old, so Mammy and Daddy had already met her. Now it was time

to meet their new granddaughter.

Daddy took one look at Brennalynn and he said, "Well

hello, my little Dowser!" Well that was it, the name stuck. That is

what my Dad was called when he was little. Dowser meant small

one or young one back in the old days and only an elder can name a Dowser in a family clan. Daddy was now a Grandfather, so it was his right to name her that. I was in absolute bliss with my parents being there! There was a sense of security and warmness that I had truly missed. Mammy and my Daddy were with me and I felt so happy. It was just so wonderful to see them with both my babies.

Even though they were with me, it did not stop Sean from acting out and continuing his bullshit. I remember one day, Daddy went out in the snow to brush off the car and put the heaters on so Sean wouldn't have to do it. Sean pulled me aside and said, "You need to tell him not to touch my car! He needs to warm it up before putting on the heaters. He will fuck up the engine."

Sean never thanked my Dad. He would just walk out and say, "See ye later."

I know that Mam and Dad were not thrilled with the situation, but they didn't bring it up to me. Mammy did notice that things were not right. They did not mention anything to me, but they knew.

One evening while they were still visiting, we went to

Anna and Bill's for dinner and my mother was very inquisitive about Sean to Anna. She kept asking Anna about his past and why he went into the Navy. That did not go down very well. Whatever the conversation was, it ended up where I heard my Mammy ask Anna," If I was to open my daughter's purse right now, how much money would be in there?"

Anna, of course did not like this question. How dare she question her son's ability to take care of his young family? There was awkwardness between them after that. My Mammy usually doesn't invite confrontations, but she tends to finish them if she was involved in one. I think it is the Murphy side of her--they are all debaters by nature.

Before I knew it, it was time for them to go back to Ireland. I was so sad to see them go. After my parents left, things just started getting out of control. Sean was gambling heavily at this time, too, and we were continually coming up short of rent money. We were discussing rehab, but he would just deny everything and lie about it.

Things just got worse and worse. The drugs were making him paranoid and irrational and just downright crazy. I came in from the store one day and was peering out the window. He said that he saw a burglar break into the townhouse across the way and he called the cops. He kept closing the blinds and locking the doors in fear of something, I don't know what, but he would be up for days.

I functioned as normally as I could with the girls, just going day-to-day. I would still cook him dinner and buy his beer to have in the fridge. I still tended to him as much as I could. This truly started to feel like a helpless situation and it bothered me so much that I was responsible for my two beautiful daughters being around this horrible, horrible situation.

I kept thinking of Nana sitting by the fire just talking about life as she pointed her finger at me, looked directly at me with her piercing blue eyes and said, "Don't you ever let a man put his hands on you! You ignore it once and it's ten times harder to stand up for yourself! Will you promise me luv? Will you?"

"I promise you Nan. I do" I replied softly.

She titled her head to the side and said,

"You won't always hear my voice Darling, but you will always know what I'm saying."

"To me Motherhood is near to spirituality. It is the highest, purest honour to be recognized by Humanity."

~ Alicia McMahon

Chapter 11

The Night It Happened

"You are a disgrace for a mother. You are nothing but a

whore. Get in the house and stop trying to draw attention

to yourself!"

When the rental lease was up on our townhouse, the
landlord would not renew it because we were always so late on
paying rent. We had to move out.

What were we going to do? We didn't have any savings, or
money, for that matter, so Sean asked his parents if we could move
into their basement. Dowser was about five months old now and I
was almost relieved that I wouldn't have to put up with all of this

215

by myself. Now they would see what he was really like and how he lied and manipulated everyone.

Boy was I wrong. Sean just kept doing what he was doing and no one questioned it. He kept gambling and doing drugs, just as much, if not more, than when we were in the rental house.

I started feeling very ill around this time and I couldn't eat much. I started losing weight. I knew there was something really wrong with me, but I was scared to even admit it to myself. Eventually, I ended up going to the doctor. He did some bloodwork and then scheduled an endoscopy. It was an ulcer. The ulcer had worked through the lining of my stomach. The pain was unbearable at times. I was barely able to do daily chores without feeling lightheaded and dizzy. I had to take medications and a special liquid that seemed to help with the pain.

We never had any money. I decided to look for a job in the evenings. I was able to get a job at Tony Roma's restaurant as a server. Physically, that was one of the hardest jobs I've ever had. I was on my feet for hours. I would usually work the 5:30 pm to close shift. It worked best for me with the girls because Anna

would be home from work and she and Bill could watch them. I

was exhausted every night, but I actually enjoyed working there. I

got to meet new friends and it distracted me from Sean and his

drug use.

I met this one girl in particular named Lindsey. She was

very pretty and about the same age as me. She had three children

and lived in Lakewood, which was about twenty-five miles away.

She and I related to each other and clicked immediately. I would

always look forward to seeing her and working during the same

shifts. I really liked her.

This one particular night it was the bartender's birthday and

he announced we were all having a beer after the restaurant closed

to celebrate. I didn't see anything wrong with it, so I stayed back

with everyone and had a beer. The weather was cold outside and

there was snow on the ground. It was 11:25 pm, which is probably

about the time we got out of there normally. I left the restaurant

about 11:45 pm and got home about 11:50 pm. I pulled up into the

driveway and went to the door to unlock it. It had been bolted from the inside, so I knocked lightly.

Then I heard Sean. "Where the fuck have you been?"

"At work, Sean. Let me in. It's snowing and freezing out here."

"No. You are not coming into this house until you tell me where you were!"

I knew by the way he was talking that he was drunk and probably drugged up.

"Sean, please open the door. It is below zero out here and I am shaking with the cold. Please! If you don't open it I will ring the doorbell and wake your parents and they will let me in!" I was sure he would open it after I said that.

"Try it and see what the fuck happens," he said through the door.

"Please open the door!"

I was pleading with him. I pushed the button and rang the doorbell. All of a sudden, the door quickly opened and Sean rushed out the storm door, which hit me in the head. I took a couple of steps backward in shock and then he charged me. I heard a muffled sound and saw a flash. He had punched me in the head on the right side. I dropped onto the snow-covered front lawn, stunned and trying to get up. He then put the bottom of his foot on my shoulder and pushed me back down. I was paralyzed with the pain and I couldn't move.

He kept saying, "Who is he? Where were you? You are off whoring around! I know you are!"

I somehow managed to get back up on my feet. I kept asking myself, *Why is he doing this?*

"What's wrong with you?"

"Please let me go inside."

He continued to throw me around like a rag doll, kicking me onto the ground until I gave up and curled up on the snow, just taking the beating. I was crying so hard, it was like a nightmare. He wouldn't stop. I found my mind kind of removing myself from my body and watching him hitting me.

I heard my Crone Voice say, *Just stay still and he will stop.* I tried so hard just to not react to getting beaten and pummeled, but it hurt so bad. I remember my hair in my mouth tasting like blood. The snow around me was a deep red color from my blood.

Then he finally stopped and said, "You are a disgrace for a mother. You are nothing but a whore. Get in the house and stop trying to draw attention to yourself."

I got up from the snow and realized I was extremely dizzy. There was a huge bulge on the side of my head and there was blood from my mouth all over the snow. I made it inside and sat on the stool by the kitchen counter. I was shaking so hard I wasn't sure if it was shock or cold from lying in the snow. Meanwhile, Sean was still calling me names, pointing his finger and pushing my face away aggressively. It was actually all muffled in my head. I couldn't make out everything he was saying and I couldn't really see him clearly.

Then, all of a sudden, something came over me. I stood up, walked back to Anna and Bill's bedroom, opened the door without knocking and said, "Anna wake up! Wake up! Please. I need your help. Get up. Sean is out of control!"

Anna got up right away, pushing me aside and walking past me as she rushed out to the living room. By this time, Sean was on the couch with his head in his hands.

"What in the hell is going on here?" Anna exclaimed.

"Sean locked me out of the house and then kept beating on me in the front lawn," I said, still trying to catch my breath and enunciate my words.

Anna looked at Sean and said, "Sean, did you? Did you put your hands on her?"

Sean looked her straight in the eyes and said, "She was asking for it. She is a lying whore and she doesn't deserve those children. She is not getting them back."

Anna looked at me and said, "Well?"

I turned and showed her my head. There was a massive goose egg by this point and there was blood splattered all over my white work shirt. My eye had started swelling up, as well, so it was obvious I had been beaten. Anna's jaw dropped and she told Sean to leave and get out.

Right at that moment, Brennalynn started crying

downstairs. Sean started to get up from the couch and I ran for the basement stairs, bolting in front of him to get my baby before he could touch her.

I was about halfway down the stairs when he grabbed my hair. I kept moving forward. He pulled a huge chunk of my hair out but I didn't care. I ran down the stairs and into the room and picked my baby up from her crib. Sean tried to grab her from me, but I wouldn't let her go. I remember feeling the scratches on my cheek from him reaching to take her from me. He was screaming in my ear and literally spitting in my face saying, "You have a whore for a mother, Brennalynn."

"She is a fucking slut!"

"She is a whore!"

It seemed like he was driven by the devil himself. He was so full of evil and so out of control.

Then as I was trying to twist out of the way of him grabbing Brennalynn, he put his hands around my neck and started squeezing really, really tight. He was choking me so hard--I will never in my life forget how that felt. I still had Brennalynn in my arms, and she started screaming like someone was pinching her or something--you know that intense hurt cry a baby makes when they are very upset or in pain? Her screaming kept me in the present moment.

Sean was squeezing harder and harder. I felt my eyes bulge and so much pressure in my ears. I was clinging to my baby, not letting her out of my arms. I kept saying in my head, *Don't let him take her, don't let him take her!* over and over again.

By this time, Anna had come into the room. She screamed and ran over to try to pull Sean's arms off my neck. She was absolutely hysterical and she was screaming at the top of her lungs trying to wake up Bill.

Sean just would not stop choking me. He was actually increasing the pressure.Anna kept yelling and hitting Sean to try to get him to stop and let me go. I felt like I was going to pass out. I saw the fairy dust on the sides of my eyes and white flashes. But I could not let him get his hands on my baby.

Anna was screaming so loud, "You are going to kill her,

Sean. Let her go. Please let go, Sean. Let her gooooo! Billll! Help! Help!"

Then I went limp. Anna must have gotten his hands off my neck. I passed out and fell on the bed with Brennalynn still in my arms. I was so dizzy and was gasping for a solid breath. I could still hear them fighting. Brennalynn's cry sounded so frightened that brought me back to reality. I rolled over and tried to calm her down and hold her in my arms.

My brain finally came back to a conscious, cognitive state. It was as if I was actually removed from my reality, but I was there. It's hard to explain. I was observing this horrible moment in time and I knew it was just one moment in time.

Trauma has a way of skewing reality. *Yeah, that's exactly how I can explain it.*

Bill physically removed Sean from the bedroom and Anna ran over to take Brennalynn from my arms. I would not let her go. Nobody was taking my child from me—

Nobody.

"Alicia, give me the baby!"

"NO! NO! NO! I have her. I'm okay," I yelled.

"You need to take a breath. Give me Brennalynn!"

"Anna! Please leave me be for a minute. Please?"

Right at that moment we heard a thump from upstairs. She turned and ran up the stairs screaming "BILL!?"

I didn't want to or care to know what was going on. All I cared about was that my baby was safe in my arms. Then panic consumed me.

Séanalee…. Séanalee? Oh, Jesus Christ Almighty, please, please don't wake up. I channeled it so strongly, almost like I knew it was going to work and she would not wake up. I heard a scuffle upstairs and I didn't know what to do. Séanalee was up there! I was downstairs. I had to go make sure my Buggie was okay. I had to go up there. I had to.

I wobbled toward the door and I held onto the wall while holding my baby in my other arm. I gradually made it to the top of the stairs. As I was walking up, I heard all the commotion.

Bill was yelling at Sean, "Where do you think you're going with that TV? If you leave this house you are not coming back."

Sean put the TV in the car and came in the back door. He went downstairs and grabbed the VCR and then left.

I immediately went to Séanalee's room. There she was, so angelic, so peaceful and beautiful and most importantly, *asleep*! I was overwhelmed. I felt like I had just dodged a bullet.

Bill locked all the doors and brought blankets out into the living room. Anna told me to try and get some sleep and she and Bill would stay upstairs to make sure Sean didn't come back.

I brought Brennalynn into bed with me. I walked towards the bed and felt my legs go out from under me, so I grabbed the bookshelf with one hand and held on to Brennalynn with the other hand.

Then I knelt down and tried to crawl to the bed. If you can picture this... I dragged her on the floor behind me until I reached the bed. I sat for a second and then lifted her up onto the bed and crawled up after her. I held her so tight and rocked her in my arms.

I felt myself lose consciousness once or twice, but I was too afraid to go upstairs to tell them. I mentally overcame the need to pass out. I had such a splitting headache. It was pounding like a heart in my head. There was so much adrenaline in me and I was in shock.

It was about an hour or two later that I heard the back gate rattle. Our room was in the basement, and there is a window-well by the gate. Then I heard footsteps on the snow and I knew he was out there.

I froze in the bed. I could not move or breathe in case he heard me. Then I heard tapping on the window.

Tap, tap, tap.

I stopped breathing, I froze. I heard my own shallow breath and that scared me. Then Sean put his head as close to the window as he could and said, "Alicia. Open the door. Let me in. I am freezing out here. I'm sorry. Now open the door, please?"

I kept the curtains closed and just pretended I couldn't hear him. My body was shaking and my teeth would not stop chattering and making noise. All I kept saying in my head was, *Please don't let him hear me!*

This went on for a couple of hours. He was crying for the last hour of it, wailing like a child who'd lost his puppy. It started to get light outside and then I heard the gate rattling again and the car starting up. Almost instantly after that, I fell asleep.

Brennalynn woke me up about 8:30 am and we went upstairs. Séanalee was already up having breakfast with Anna and Bill. Anna said they were going to church and I should try to get more rest.

My face and head were swollen beyond what I can honestly describe here. I had blood crusted on the sides of my mouth and both my eyes were blood-filled with no white to be seen. I jumped in the shower to get the blood off my body and rushed back out to the sitting room in case anything happened.

After an hour or so, they left for church and I took Brennalynn downstairs to try and take a nap. I fell asleep almost right away.

When I opened my eyes, there was Sean, standing right by my bed.

Was I dreaming? Was this real? My heart stopped and froze for a second. He was just standing there and looking at me.

"How did you get in?" I asked.

"I took the wire grate off the sliding glass door and took off the door," he replied.

I was paralyzed with fear. I was so afraid for my life at that moment--even more than the previous night. I felt the danger. I knew he was still drugged up on something and the rage I saw in his eyes will never leave my head.

"Come on, get up, I am taking you out for breakfast," he said casually.

"No, Sean, I'm tired and I already ate," I said.

He looked at me very peculiarly and said, "Come on. I have money."

I really did not want to get him worked up again, so I got up and put some sweat pants and a sweatshirt on. I realized I had very obvious bruises on my neck. I also had a burst blood vessels in my eyes and my right cheekbone was swollen. I looked pretty bad, to be honest with you. I covered everything I could and dressed and changed Brennalynn.

Sean was acting completely normal, as if nothing had happened. It was so bizarre. We went to breakfast and he ordered two country breakfasts and coffee.

While we were waiting for our food he said, "All you had to do is tell me the truth and this wouldn't have happened."

I felt like I needed to throw up. My body must have been having a reaction to the trauma. I honestly could not believe he had said that. He just kept talking through breakfast and I was still in a haze. He even started playing with Brennalynn, saying, "Give your Daddy a smile." Needless to say, she didn't.

I really couldn't eat anything, so Sean ate my breakfast as well as his own. As I watched him sitting across from me, it was like I was in a different world.

Was I going crazy? was this real? Was I here sitting across from a man who just tried to kill his wife in a drug-induced rage?

I looked at his face as all of this kept going through my mind. It was almost like I was watching everything from above the table where we were eating. It was like a separation of reality.

Just hazy. Everything was hazy.

When he was done, he brought us back to the house. He didn't come in and just said he was going to his sister Nora's place. I knew he had gone to her house before to use crack, so I was not surprised he was headed there. I was very relieved he was not coming in. He knew his Mother and Father wouldn't be happy to see him and he was well used to avoiding them.

Anna and Bill came home soon after. I heard the front door open, so I walked up the stairs and I turned the corner to get Séanalee.

Anna was standing there and said, "Sit down, Alicia. I was talking to my sister Reba and she said that we need to bring you to a safe place until he calms down. We can't protect you or the girls from him right now."

Reba had already called a safehouse in Boulder. They said I had to pack and hurry before he came back. I grabbed what I could in a pure, blind panic.

I wasn't questioning a thing. I almost felt saved. We packed the car, grabbed the children and Anna drove us into Boulder. We had to meet at the courthouse at 6th and Canyon. I could tell that Anna was genuinely scared of what would happen, but something inside her knew she had to do this.

When we pulled into the courthouse, there was a car there with a woman inside it. She saw us pull up and got out. She approached our car, put out her hand and we shook hands. She introduced herself as Roxanne. She asked Anna if I had any bags and immediately started loading them into her car.

Anna asked where the safehouse was, but Roxanne looked at Anna and said, "Nobody knows where the safehouse is. Otherwise, it would not be a *safehouse*. Then Anna wanted a phone number, and again Roxanne said, "No, that is also against the rules."

The exchange was actually very formal, and I don't think Anna liked it. Anna kept trying to tell Roxanne that this was just temporary until things cooled down. We transferred the children into Roxanne's car and said our goodbyes. I got into Roxanne's car and strapped in Brennalynn and Séanalee, and then I looked back at Anna, who was standing there waving at us.

It felt like I was back at the Limerick City train station all over again. It was the same feeling as when I was leaving Ireland and headed to America. It felt so good to be out of that horrible, sick, dirty, negative environment.

I felt like I could breathe, like I had a huge cloud lifted from over my head. I recalled Nana's words in that moment and I knew I was going to be safe now. "Don't you ever let a man put his hands on you! You ignore it once and it's ten times harder to stand up for yourself! And follow your heart, luv. It already knows the road and path ahead."

"Courage doesn't always roar.

Sometimes courage is the quiet voice that will not stop

pushing you."

~ Alicia McMahon

Chapter 12

The Safehouse

"You will be fine, Lysh, I promise.

You are my daughter and you are tough! You're a Mc!"

We arrived at the safehouse, which was a very nice

Victorian home nestled at the base of the foothills in Boulder. It

didn't look like what I thought a *safehouse* would look like. It was

in a very nice neighborhood and looked like a normal home. They

showed us around the house. There was a big den where most of

the women and children hung out in a communal area. The kitchen

234

was big, too. It had two sets of tables and chairs and a little dining room off the kitchen which had a beautiful bay window.

They showed us to our room and explained the rules of the house and the cooking and cleaning schedule. It was all barter. We were sharing the bedroom with another woman and her son. I had bunk beds and a playpen for Brennalynn to sleep in at the end of my bed.

It was tight quarters, but we didn't mind at all. We put our stuff away and then Roxanne came in and explained the rules of the shelter. There were six other women with their children living in the house. We all had chores to do. We took turns making dinner and we had to keep our rooms tidy at all times. We had to sign out if we left the house and I could not leave the children unattended, ever. We had to meet with our counselor each day and attend group meetings three times a week.

After we went over the list, Roxanne told me I needed to come and do an intake interview with her, which was essentially an assessment of my situation. She had volunteers play with the girls while I went into the office. I went in and sat down. Roxanne closed the door sat down across from me and held both my hands in hers. She said, "Take a deep breath. You are safe now." I think perhaps I was still a little bit in shock. I was still shaking inside, so I did take a deep breath and it felt good.

The first thing Roxanne noticed were the marks on my neck. She took a picture of the bruising. Then she started asking me questions about my relationship with Sean. She was writing in her notepad as we were talking. After about an hour, the interview was complete and she put the notepad away. She asked me if I thought I was in an abusive relationship. That was easy for me to answer because I still had bruises on me and red in my eyes. But I truly did not grasp the severity of being in an abusive relationship with someone who had an addiction. She helped me understand in that first session that there was nothing I could have done to fix this, no matter what anyone said.

That night seemed endless. Once we were done with the entire paperwork and intake interview, I set up our beds and drawers in the bedroom.

I laid down in the bed with Séanalee and her arms immediately reached out for me. She didn't know what was going on, only that she felt out of her comfort zone. There was another family, a Mom and baby, in our room, and I felt really bad trying to comfort my girls in front of a stranger.

Brennalynn would not let me out of her sight. She was so clingy and scared. I eventually got both girls to lay with me in bed and all three of us held each other that night. I listened to their breathing. It was so reassuring to have them so close and with me. I stared at the bunk bed mattress directly above us and dreamed of the girls and me going home to my family in Ireland. Nobody would hurt us there. It would be the exact opposite, as a matter of fact. We would be loved, kissed and hugged every day.

I don't think I completely comprehended exactly what was going on for about a week. I would watch the other women get in their cars and go shopping to the store. They had vehicles and means of transportation. They had very structured days there.

I really didn't know how I was going to get through this, but I knew I had to. Then I remembered my Daddy's words, "You will be fine, Lysh, I promise. You are my daughter and you are tough! You're a Mc!"

I only had two or three weeks to go and I could go home to Ireland. Tina and Gerard were getting married the week after Christmas and I was her Matron of Honour. She had bought me and the girls tickets to Ireland months earlier.

The only thing was, I had left them at Anna and Bill's house. I was in such shock and dismay that I'd completely forgot to get my passport and tickets. I did, however, hide them in the bookcase downstairs. I could not tell you why I did that – I just did. I told the safehouse that I just want to go home and be with my family. They helped figure out how to change the date of the flight.

Roxanne said she had seen this before and she called the airline and got the tickets changed without any penalty fee. She explained the situation to the airline and called it a "special domestic violence situation." She also arranged for me to go to Anna and Bill's house and get my passport and tickets with an escort from the Adams County Sheriff. I felt somewhat empowered and in control for the first time in a long while. I also had to call Tony Roma's where I worked and tell them I was unable to continue working there.

Anna had called the main safehouse number and checked in with me a few times. She kept asking me when I was coming back, and I kept telling her I didn't know. Then she asked me if I was planning to go back to Ireland and to that, I said, "I don't know." She still had a way of making me feel inadequate, even when I was safe and away from her drug-addicted, wife-beating son.

She said, "It's not good for the girls to be away from their father. You have had time to cool off, Alicia. Now it's time to come back."

As soon as I mentioned to Anna that I needed to get some things from the house, she pretty much turned on me.

She kept saying, "Tell me what you want and I will bring it to you."

I didn't want her to know that I hid the passports in the bookcase. I also did not want her to know that I just wanted to go

239

home. I told her there was going to be a sheriff coming with me to make sure Sean wouldn't try anything. She sounded very angry and frustrated with me over the phone and she hung up on me.

We had arranged to go get my documents and the girls' passports the next day. Roxanne drove me to Westminster and we parked a little away from the house and waited for the sheriff.

Roxanne told me to not waste time and not to reply or respond to anything. I was to go in, get what I needed and leave. We saw the sheriff pull up and I felt my stomach go instantly sour. I wanted to throw up as soon as I saw the house. A rush of emotions came over me and I felt my face flush. Roxanne put her hand on mine, looked me in the eye and said, "You can do this, Alicia. Don't feel bad about it."

So we go out of the car and Roxanne introduced herself and me to the sheriff. He explained he was there just to ensure I got what was mine and I didn't encounter any resistance. We walked up and the sheriff sternly knocked on the door.

Bill opened it and said, "Can I help you?" Just then he saw

me and stepped aside, opening the door wider.

The sheriff said, "This isn't going to take long. Alicia is just grabbing her belongings and leaving."

Then Anna said, "Can I see what she takes to make sure it does belong to her?"

The sheriff replied, "I don't see why not. Are you okay with that, Alicia?"

I said "Yes," but I knew she just wanted to see what I was coming to get. I went downstairs and went straight for the bookcase, grabbing our passports and tickets. I also found $40 in there, which I didn't remember putting in the front page of Séanalee's passport. I needed it and it was a nice surprise. I had the passports, the tickets and $40 in an envelope. I looked around the room and grabbed Brennalynn's blankie and a couple more doe-doe's that were in her cot. I also saw a scarf and a little photo album that I picked up on my way out of the bedroom. I walked upstairs with the items and said, "Okay, let's go!"

Anna immediately said, "I want to see what you took."

I went through what was in my hands one by one and

showed her.

Then she said, "Well, I bought that photo album."

I looked at her and said, "Okay, I guess that is yours," and I put it on the counter. Then she asked, "What is in the envelope?" I pulled out the passports and my green card and our tickets home. She looked at Bill and then looked back at me with loathing in her eyes.

Then the sheriff asked, "Did you get all you needed, Mrs. Flatley?"

I replied, "Yes. Can we go now, please?"

As I walked out, Roxanne tapped me on the back and said, "You did great, Alicia."

We thanked the sheriff and headed back to the safehouse. I was trying to figure out how I felt. Exhilarated? Sad? Happy? Scared? I knew one thing--I really wanted to throw up. I had a blunt pain in my stomach and I felt green at the gills.

Now, since we had changed the airline tickets to the day before, I had to face calling home and telling them I was in a battered women's shelter. I was trying to avoid telling my family at home because I didn't want them to worry. I just wanted to get home safe and sound. I gave Séanalee and Brennalynn a bath, fed them dinner and read *The Ugly Duckling* storybook they loved. Séanalee was not as tired so I sang *You are My Sunshine* to her and rocked her to sleep.

Usually you can make phone calls on the pay phone, but because this was an international call, they allowed me to use their phone in the counselor's office instead. I collected myself as much as I could, so I could be matter-of-fact and not an emotional mess when I called.

Gale and Roxanna left the office so I could make the call. I took a deep breath, picked up the phone and dialed Mammy and Daddy's number in Mount David. Amy picked up. She was so happy to hear my voice and was excited.

I would be home soon. She was asking me a ton of questions.

I interrupted her and said, "Amy, is Tina there?"

She replied with, "Yeah, Lysha, I'll get her for you. I love you. I can't wait to see you next week."

She put the phone on the counter and called Tina. I heard Tina walking on the tiles into the kitchen. She picked up the phone and said, "Well, how's she cuttin', sister?" I could hear the excitement in her voice, too, and then all of a sudden, I lost all my composure.

"Tina, make sure you are alone. I need to talk to you." My voice was shaking, I was obviously upset.

She asked Amy to leave the kitchen. Amy was only nine or ten years old and she was used to being asked to leave the room, so she didn't suspect anything. Tina came back on the phone and directly asked, "What's happened, Lysh? What's going on?"

I tried to be nonchalant and seem like I was in control.

"Don't tell anyone this, but I am in a safehouse in Boulder. I got my ticket changed to the 11th, so I will be flying in a day earlier than planned. I will talk with the family as soon as I get home. I just don't want anyone to worry. Can you come pick us up at the airport?"

244

"Oh My God! Jesus Christ…of course, I will! You need to let me know what happened! Why are you there? What is a safehouse? Lysh, what the fuck is going on?"

"A safehouse is a place for battered women and children. Sean just lost it, Teen. He is crazy and out of control. He tried to strangle me. He was trying to kill me. He has been on drugs for a while and it's a very bad situation. I am safe and the girls are fine. We will stay here until the flight. Please, please, Tina, don't tell Mammy and Daddy. Don't tell anyone."

"Jesus Christ Almighty, Alicia! Okay, just keep me posted and I will meet you at the airport. Stay strong, sister," she said in a panicked voice.

"I will, Teen," I answered. "I love you so much and I'll see you next week."

I hung up the phone. I felt somewhat better, maybe because I had shared my misery and knew I was going home to the arms of my family.

A couple more days passed, and I was definitely feeling a little better. I was sweeping up the kitchen as one of my chores when one of the other women called me and said that there was a message on the notice board for me. I didn't know we had a notice board for messages. There was a message for *Irish Alisha* which read:

Where are you? Please call me.

Lindsey – at Tony Roma's

I knew it couldn't be anyone else but me. I did remember Lindsey, but why would she be looking for me? I called the restaurant and left a message for her. We were not allowed to receive phone calls on the public phone, although we could make phone calls. So, the next day there was another message from Lindsey to call her back. This time she left her phone number. I called her later that night, once the girls were sleeping. She was so concerned about me. It took me back a bit. She said, "I have been calling all the women's shelters around Denver, Westminster, Arvada and Boulder leaving messages with all of them. Are you okay?"

"I'm fine. You're so nice to be worried about me," I said

genuinely.

"I couldn't sleep at all after I heard you weren't coming back and you went to a women's shelter. I just knew I liked you a lot and I wanted to make sure you were okay. I know you don't have family over here."

I couldn't believe someone was concerned enough to call around to numerous shelters looking for me. After talking on the phone a few times, she even came up to Boulder to see us and we would take the girls for a walk and go to the park to play with them. I was so happy Lindsey was in my life. She lived in Lakewood, which was south of Denver, so traveling up to Boulder took about forty-five-minutes-to-an-hour's drive.

Lindsey even offered to drive me to the airport on the day I was going home. I was so grateful to have her as a friend. She would come to Boulder and pick me up and bring me down to Lakewood for the day to her apartment to spend the day with her husband and three kids and then drive me all the way back to Boulder.

Finally, the day came for me to go home! I was so excited.

I just wanted my family, hugs and kisses. I had packed up everything I had, gave Séanalee and Brennalynn baths, put their hair up in bows and put on nice clean clothes. I had to do an exit interview with the safehouse and then Roxanne was going to drop me off at the courthouse to meet Lindsey. I couldn't believe I was actually going to breathe and be safe and sound.

We pulled up at the courthouse and there was Lindsey with her little red Geo Metro car. Roxanne helped me transfer the luggage and little Buggy into the boot of Lindsay's car. Lindsey already had a car seat from her kids, so we strapped Brennalynn into that, buckled up Séanalee and we were set!

I turned to say goodbye and thanked Roxanne for all that she had done. She had her arms open for a hug. I reciprocated and found I couldn't hold back my emotions. I just started crying. It was the weirdest thing. I found myself unable to control the rush of sadness, happiness, loneliness and appreciation, all at once. I couldn't control the burst of emotion.

I was so excited to finally be on the road home! I was in great form, laughing and joking on the way to the airport. It was about an hour's drive to Denver International Airport before we pulled into the parking lot. Lindsey got out and came in with us. I was a bit nervous because I didn't have our physical tickets--just the original ones for us to leave the next day.

I walked up to the ticket counter and gave the lady my tickets. she looked at them and said, "These are for tomorrow."

"Yes Ma'am I know," I replied. "The director of the Boulder Women's Shelter called yesterday and the airline gave me an exception to change them under special circumstances."

The woman looked a bit puzzled and asked me to wait there. She talked to her supervisor and they came back to the computer and looked up my tickets. There was indeed a special circumstance added to the notes. They changed our tickets, took my bag, put the luggage tag on it and put it on the belt. I had our new tickets in hand. I looked at Lindsey and I said, "I can't believe it. We're going home!"

Lindsey walked me to the security point and gave me the

biggest, tightest hug and said, "Go home and be safe, Alicia. It's time to start your next chapter in life."

I kissed Lindsey on the cheek and told her I would never forget what she'd done for us and that I loved her. I rolled Brennalynn onto the train in a stroller while holding Séanalee's hand and waved to Lindsey as the doors closed. As the train picked up speed, I had a hard time holding onto Séanalee while keeping Brennalynn steady in her stroller.

All of sudden I heard, "Lysha!"

The voice sounded aggressive. However, only people I know call me by my nickname, so I turned around. There was a man standing in front of me wearing a loud, colorful, short-sleeved Hawaiian shirt. He looked me in the eyes and asked, "Alicia Flatley?"

"Yes" I replied, completely confused.

He said his name and said that he was a private investigator. Then handed me an envelope and stated, "You have been served."

I didn't know what was going on, so I turned around to ignore him as much as I could in a crowded train. I started shaking inside. I didn't want my babies to see me frightened. We had one more terminal to go and it was our stop to catch our plane home to Ireland.

The man approached me again and said, "Do you know what this means? You cannot take those children out of the state of Colorado, never mind taking them out of the country. If you get on that plane you WILL be arrested."

Everyone's eyes were set on me, and the stares were somewhat accusatory, as if I had done something criminal. I didn't know what was in the manila envelope and there was some part of me that never wanted to know. I started crying. I couldn't help it. I looked back at him and yelled, "Sir, please leave me alone and stop following me!"

The train stopped, I rushed out with the girls, glancing behind me to see if the man got off the train too. Of course, he did. I rushed into the crowd and went straight into the bathroom. I sat up against the wall. I put Séanalee between my legs to make sure she didn't run off and kept Brennalynn in the stroller beside us.

I took a deep breath and then I opened the envelope and pulled out a stack of pages separated into packets. There was a Colorado Court seal near the top of the first page. They were court papers. The first packet had *Dissolution of Marriage* on it and the second had *Emergency Injunction*. English is my first language, but the words seemed so foreign to me. I didn't quite understand it, but I did read that it stated that I could not leave the State of Colorado because there was a court date.

I didn't know what to do. I was so afraid, and I was only steps away from the plane that would take me and my children home for good. I was in the bathroom for about forty-five minutes fighting my fear, trying to make sense of what all of this meant. I debated if I should just make a run for it and jump on the plane and never look back or confront the man. I peered out the door to find where my gate was and saw the private investigator standing there with two police officers. They were talking with the gate agent.

I watched them for a minute and then they all went on the

plane. Oh, dear Mother of God, they were looking for me! I was so glad I hadn't gotten onto the plane. Can you just imagine? There were two police officers holding up an airplane to search it for me? I said, *enough is enough.*

I walked over to the gate with the girls and approached the first officer. "Are you looking for me? My name is Alicia Flatley." I had a quiver in my voice due to raw emotion.

The police officer turned around and said, "Yes, we are." He approached me and directed me to walk with him away from the gate. I was holding Séanalee in my arm and pushing Brennalynn while holding the diaper bag and my handbag. He stated his name and said that the private investigator thought I went on the plane. They had intended to arrest me if I had attempted to take the children out of the state.

I started crying, and panic racing in my heart. I told the officer I didn't know what to do. I told him the safehouse had gotten my tickets changed and I didn't know where to go.

The officer asked me if I understood what the papers I was served meant and I said, "No." He told me Sean had filed for a divorce and had also asked the Judge to issue an emergency injunction to stop me from leaving the state with the children until the divorce hearing was complete.

The officer looked at me with kind eyes and said, "Ma'am, I want you to know I am not judging you. I know all you want is to go home to your family. This is procedure. You are not in any trouble right now."

The private investigator and the other police officer walked over and confirmed we were not on the plane. I had thirteen dollars in my pocket, Dowser's nappy bag with nappies, wipes, juice, crackers and a pair of leggings for both of the girls. I really didn't know what to do.

Again, I sat on the floor and tried to figure it out. What should I do? How could I deal with this? How could I get home? That's all that was going through my head.

It dawned on me--I was in trouble.

How could I deal with this? Then I remembered how I had overcome so much worse than this and I reflected for a minute. I distracted the girls and gave them both a snack bag of goldfish crackers.

I closed my eyes, took a deep breath and just…reflected. I was feeling, oddly enough…confident. I had a realization about how I'd gotten here.

As a teenager, I'd worked, fought and strived from early in the morning until late at night to find my dream.

I'd overcome the fucken thug in England who almost stifled me.

I'd overcome that horrible, awful situation of being abused, beat and strangled. So, after looking back on my life thus far and how I'd gotten here, I realized I was now the Mammy. I was Séanalee and Brennalynn's Mammy.

I knew I could do this! I could do this! My Crone Voice decided to allow me to narrate this one.

I've got this! Right? Yes, I've got this!

I went to the phone booth in the airport, called the operator and asked to make a collect call to Ireland. Tina picked up the phone and I immediately started crying.

"Lysh, where are you?" she exclaimed.

"Oh, Tina! I am still in Denver at the airport. They had a private investigator follow me and serve me with papers saying I can't leave. My bag is on the plane, Teen, and I have no money. I don't know what to do."

"What the fuck! Are you joken me? Are you okay? Are my nieces okay?" she asked.

By that time, I heard Mam and Dad in the background and I told Tina she would have to talk to them and explain what had happened. She would also have to find someone else to step in for me as Matron of Honour for her wedding in a few days.

She said she would call Gerard, her fiancé in New York, and have him wire me some money to the Western Union in Boulder. She told me to call the safehouse and let them know what had happened and then call my friend Lindsey and ask her to come back and get me and the girls.

I called the safehouse and told them I was stopped at the

airport by a private investigator and that he had served me with papers. I didn't know what to do or where to go. They said it might be too risky to come back to the safehouse because no one could know the location. Roxanne asked me to see if I could stay with a friend for a day or so until I was positive that I wasn't being followed back to the shelter. I said, "All right, I'll call Lindsey now."

"Alicia, we'll help you get through this," Roxanne said. "Just make sure you are not followed back by anyone and call me back once you are in a safe place."

"Okay, Roxanne, I will!"

I called Lindsey and thank God she was at her house. I let her know what was going on and what had just happened.

She said, "I'll meet you at passenger pick-up in twenty minutes."

I fed Brennalynn and Séanalee, changed Brennalynn's nappy and made my way out to passenger pick-up. I was only standing there about two minutes when Lindsey pulled up.

She ran out of the car and hugged me, saying, "Okay, we

have to get going. I won't bring you back to my house. We can go to my Aunt's. She'll help us."

We got the girls in the car and took off. I was shaking so bad I couldn't control it. She drove into the parking structure and then drove on every floor to make sure we were not being followed. Even after parking the car, we waited for about ten minutes, carefully looking around before we headed out to her Aunt's house.

When we arrived, we got out of the car and went into the house. Her Aunt Brenda was home when Lindsey and I walked in with the girls. Lindsey had called her after we'd spoken at the airport. I'd never met her before, but she greeted me with a big hug.

"Now," she said, "sit down. I have coffee made and you can tell me what happened."

I went through the series of events and told her everything. She asked, "Would you mind if I took a look at those papers?"

"Oh, yes, please do," I replied.

I gave her the envelope and she explained to me that Sean had filed for divorce in order to stop me from taking the girls back to Ireland. She also explained they had requested an emergency injunction and Anna and Bill were third-party interveners in the case.

"What does that mean?" I asked.

"Sean has an attorney, and Anna and Bill also have an attorney. The only way they could stop you from leaving was to file for a divorce and also ask a judge to make you stay here until the custody of the girls is decided on. It says here they believed you were not coming back from Ireland with their grandchildren."

Wow. I just realized what all this meant. I was in for a fight for my children.

Brenda handed me the phone and told me to call my parents in Ireland and tell them I was safe here and she would bring me back to the safehouse tomorrow.

So, I called Mount David and Mammy picked up the phone. "Darling, darling, what is going on?" she asked me in disbelief.

"Did Tina tell you, Mam? That the girls and I have been in a shelter for a couple of weeks?"

"She did. I don't know why you wouldn't tell us Lysh. You are my daughter," she said.

"I thought I would be coming home for good Mammy. I was planning on telling ye everything once I got there. But now they have stopped me from bringing the girls out of the state of Colorado. Sean filed for divorce to stop me and there is an injunction in place. Bill and Anna have their own lawyer, Mam, and I don't know what to do," I explained.

"Jesus Christ Almighty, Alicia, how could they do this to you? Tina told me he tried to kill you. Is that true?"

"He has been on drugs for a while, Mammy. He lost his mind. He beat me up pretty bad and even tried to choke me and I passed out. Anna was trying to pull him off me. I was brought to a battered women's shelter in Boulder. It's called a safehouse."

Daddy came on the other line and said, "They can't stop you from coming home, Lysh. We're your family."

"They can, Daddy, and they did," I said.

"THEY CAN'T FUCKEN DO THAT. WE ARE YOUR BLOOD!" He had such desperation in his voice. I'd never heard that from Daddy before.

I picked up how devastating it was for them to try to understand and comprehend what was happening. "Listen, I will be fine. I will figure out how to deal with this and then I will be home for good. Okay? Don't worry about anything, sure, aren't I as tough as old boots?" I said.

"That you are! Lysh, you are my daughter, you are a Mc," Daddy said sternly.

"I love ye. I will call ye and talk tomorrow. Can you put Tina on, Mammy?" I asked.

"I will luv. I love you so, so much. Stay safe, Alicia. Here she is, luv…"

"Lysha, do you have a pen and paper? I want you to take down Gerard's mobile number. He is in New York for another couple of days before he comes here for the wedding," she said.

"I do, Teen, go ahead."

"Call him now, Lysh. He has some money for you and he needs details on where to send it."

"Okay, Teen, I will. I love you!"

"I love you too, little sister! Call us tomorrow with an update."

"I will, Tina. Bye."

Then I called Gerard in New York and explained the story. He wired me $250 to the Boulder King Soopers grocery store through Western Union and told me if it wasn't enough to call him in Ireland after Friday. He had such anger in his voice when he said, "They are nothing but a pack of fucken ignorant bastards. You will be okay, Alicia. You mind those girls and we will talk soon."

"Okay. Thanks so much, Gerard," I said, with tears in my eyes. I was so grateful for him.

I stayed the night at Brenda's house. Lindsey came back for us in the morning and drove us to the King Soopers, where I got the money Gerard had wired to me. I called Roxanna and she met

Lindsey and I at the usual drop off/pick up spot, the Boulder County Courthouse. Lindsey handed me a Christmas card from her Aunt Brenda. there was a $100 bill inside. I felt so grateful and sad at the same time. Why would someone just hand over their money to a complete stranger?

I had a little breakdown crying session privately. My chest hurt with gratitude, ya know what I mean? I will never forget the kindness they showed me. I want someone else to feel what I felt when they gave that to me.

That was one of the *note to self* times for me in my life, to strive to be kind. We got out of the car and again transferred the girls into Roxanna's car and she drove us to the safehouse.

After I got the girls to bed that night, I went down to the counselor's office and spoke with Gale and Roxanna. I showed them the papers I was served and they went over some of my options. They had already found an attorney who would represent me pro bono. Her name was Katherine King. I can't get over how much people help each other. Now I had a lawyer who would not charge me any money. I felt so grateful and happy. I was so afraid the Flatley's would do what they did best and bully me.

I had to meet Ms. King on Friday and I didn't have any clothes to wear that were appropriate, so the safehouse counselors gave me coupons to the local thrift store to buy some clothes for the girls and me. Gale had mentioned there was a time limit to how long you could stay at the safehouse, but she had requested that it not apply to me due to special circumstances and it was approved. I felt so relieved. It was like a wave of good feelings and energy just encompassed my entire body. She also told me I could apply for an apartment through them and it would be a two-year lease that would only charge me 1/3 of my income, regardless of how much I made, so I would need to get a job. There were six other families applying for the same apartment, so I needed to write a letter to the director and explain my situation. As I was writing that letter my entire situation became that much more real to me.

What if I didn't get it? Where would I go? What would I do?

I submitted my application and letter to the Boulder County

Outreach Director and anxiously waited to hear back. It was the longest four days ever. Gale called me in to the office and announced that I got the apartment and I could move in at the end of the month. She also gave me a $200 voucher for a second-hand thrift store to get some household stuff and she also let me know I was on a list to get furniture donations.

WOW!

I didn't feel as overwhelmed and instead felt my life was becoming more manageable. I kept thinking in my head, *We are going to be okay, we are going to be okay, we are going to be okay!*

It was hard to comprehend it.

I had my own home!

I would make it so pretty and the girls would have their own space. We would be together all the time.

I had $250 to my name and I had a list of programs I was going to apply to. I needed to get us back on our feet. I needed help in finding childcare, food and maybe even some help with clothes and shoes.

The next morning, I woke up earlier than usual and woke the girls up, too. We were all washed and dressed before 7:15 am. For breakfast, we had the usual--Brennalynn had toast and an egg in a cup and Séanalee had porridge with a splash of maple syrup.

My tummy was kind of nervous that day, so I just had coffee. I put hats, scarfs and coats on both girls and then walked to the bus stop. It was snowing like crazy. My fingers were frozen pushing the buggy to the bus.

I took the bus to the Boulder County building and applied for food stamps and AFDC. I found out that because I was not a citizen of the US I wasn't entitled to food stamps, but both the girls were. AFDC is a program where I got a check each week and the government went after Sean and either put a wage assignment on him or billed him directly. I also applied for CHP, which was health care for the girls, and for day care assistance. I felt productive and in control--complete control, as a matter of fact. It was me, myself, I, mise, mé féin, my own self, who was in charge of our destiny and there was no one who was going to dictate what we did. I think I got used to not having much of a say, or if I did have a say about anything, it would be dismissed immediately.

I had an appointment with my lawyer. Katherine and I went into downtown Boulder with the girls. Her office was on the corner of Broadway and Pearl Street right in heart of the Pearl Street Mall. We went in and sat down in her office for an update. She told me I had a court date in a couple of weeks and at the same time we were going to file for a permanent restraining order against Sean.

She also explained to me that we were going to ask that they allowed me to go home to visit my family and have them pay for the tickets. She drafted a response to the cases, the divorce, the injunction, the restraining order and the child support order.

I met her the following Tuesday and signed the documents and she filed them with the court. I wasn't quite sure how I felt, exactly. It was more than relief--more like sheer happiness and a sense of impending freedom.

There was something good on the horizon. I could feel it in my bones.

A couple of days later, Roxanna called me into the office

and told me Anna had called them and said she thought it was time for me to go back. That I just needed a *cooling off* period and Sean said he would do better. She asked me how I felt about that.

I said, "I don't want to go back there. I don't want to raise my children in that environment!"

There was no hesitancy in my reply and I felt very strongly about this. No way was I going to allow that to happen.

Roxanna said she hoped I would stay strong and do the best thing for my girls and myself. Then she mentioned that Anna had said I had a drinking problem and she was worried about my ability to mind and take care of my children. I could NOT believe what I was hearing. Why would she say something like that? She also told me Anna also said she felt like I was being brainwashed by them and being told what to do. That day I realized how deceptive people could really be and I promised myself never to forget what she was capable of…NEVER!

Christmas morning was nice, though a bit weird, but the kids were having fun. The safehouse had a gift for everyone living there so it felt really warm. They did not have a tree, though, which at that time felt strange to me. So Séanalee and Brennalynn got to open a gift. Brennalynn got a colouring book and crayons and Séanalee got a little brush set. I opened my gift and it was a lovely teacup that said "Dream" on it. I still have that teacup today.

We had just finished opening the gifts when the police showed up at the door. Jon Benet Ramsey had been murdered, and their house was a block and a half away from the safehouse. The police were asking if anyone had seen or heard anything at all the previous night.

I will never forget that morning. I kept thinking that I had my two little girls a block away from where an intruder entered a house and killed a child. This was a very affluent part of Boulder, certainly not the ghetto. How could something like this happen? I even questioned myself if I had what it took to protect my girls from something like this.

Then I realized YES! I would die before I would allow anyone to hurt my children. Full stop. That day stuck with me and is still an important day in my life. I concluded that day that I was all my children had and it was 100% my responsibility to protect them from the nastiness and evil in the world. I have never questioned it since that day. Having gone through the scary times and ending up independent with my babies gave me a certain confidence I don't think I would have ever felt if we hadn't gone through what we did.

On the day of court, I was nervous, yet strangely confident. I met with my lawyer out in front of the courthouse and stayed by her side. I was just so nervous to see Sean. I felt a dull, blunt pain in my stomach. I didn't ever want to look at his face again. I found even the image of him was making me feel ill.

We walked into the courthouse and then into the courtroom. I looked to the left of the chairs and there he was.

UGH...My stomach dropped! I felt like I wanted to throw up right there and then. I instantly remembered the feeling of his hands around my neck and looking into his eyes and seeing evil staring right back at me. Anna, Bill and Mike, his brother, were also there. I didn't even look at them.

The judge called our case and Katherine and I stepped up, as did Sean and his attorney. The judge asked about the response to the injunction first and Katherine explained that I had tickets to my sister's wedding that had been purchased a couple of months ago and the Flatley's were aware of this. She asked the judge if he could lift the injunction to allow me to go home for what was left of the holidays and see my family with the promise that I would return and finish up with the proceedings. The judge agreed and asked them to pay for the new tickets. The judge then addressed the restraining order and put Sean on the stand. He admitted to trying to choke me and said it only happened one time. He was such a liar! I think the judge knew he was lying.

Then the judge brought me up to the stand and asked me if this had happened before. I said yes, he had beaten me before, but I was afraid for my life that night. He violently beat me, kicked me and tried to strangle me while I was holding my baby. I didn't tell the judge about every time it had happened, but I did say I was abused and beaten multiple times.

The judge issued a permanent restraining order.

That was it! He couldn't contact me or be within one-hundred feet of me ever again! It was an unusual feeling I experienced at that moment--so relieved, happy, afraid and guilty all at the same time.

Relieved because I knew he couldn't hurt me anymore.

Happy because now I could go home and see my family.

Afraid because I knew that they would not let this go and would attempt to manipulate me again.

Guilty because…I don't know. It may have been the battered woman in me at that time. But I was definitely feeling guilty.

I had to meet with Katherine again the next day. She went over how the divorce was going to work. She also mentioned that they would have to buy my tickets by the end of the week. Even though I would miss my sister's wedding, I would finally get to see everyone. She told me the Flatley's attorney had contacted her and asked if they could see the girls and that there were no restraining orders against them, just with their father and me.

I told Katherine that I was really nervous about that and I did not want him to be around the girls if he was on drugs. She drafted up an agreement that would allow the girls visit their grandparents only if I had a urine analysis to prove Sean was not taking drugs. I would also get to call in two screenings a month at random. I said they could see the girls this week for a few hours, but I was so upset inside. I really did not want my girls to have any contact with them until I knew they would be safe. I knew Séanalee wanted to see her grandparents and Dowser had just turned one and she probably would like to go also, so I agreed. Thank God the visit went without incident.

New Year's Eve night came around and Brennalynn had a bad cough. It was one of those deep coughs and I knew it didn't sound right. She would get fits of coughing. A couple of times she could not catch her breath.

I knew I had to bring her to the doctor. I packed up the girls and put their coats on and walked to the bus to go to the doctor's office. We were in the waiting room for an hour-and-forty-five minutes.

They finally called us in to see the doctor and he said that she had a form of croup and an ear infection, so they gave me a prescription to put her on antibiotics. I felt so bad for my little baby. She was so sick.

I walked to the pharmacy in the snow with Brennalynn in her stroller and Séanalee holding onto the handle. We struggled with every step. It was really hard to maneuver us through almost two feet of snow for about a mile-and-a-half. I was sweating and a little emotional after our journey to get to the doctor's office, waiting that long and then being told that my little baby was so sick. My heart was aching and I just wanted to stop pushing the stroller and sit on a bench and cry my eyes out, but I didn't. I knew I had to just push on and get her the antibiotics and get everyone back to the safehouse to warm up and eat some supper.

I was so relieved when we got home. I gave Brennalynn her medicine as soon as we walked in the door. I was starting to feel better now that she had the antibiotics. We all got into warm pajamas and I made some hot soup, bread and butter and tea for supper.

The next day was New Year's day and she woke up with a rash all over her body and was visibly struggling to breath. I panicked and ran directly to Gale and showed her the rash. She told me I might want to take her to the emergency room.

My heart sank into my feet. My poor, poor Dowser. I was scared and didn't know how to get her to the emergency room. I didn't know where the hospital was. I brought her back into our bedroom and got her dressed and bundled up. She would not stop crying--screaming crying. It was so upsetting to hear. Then I put Dowser on the floor and bundled up Séanalee. I grabbed my jacket, picked up Brennalynn and holding Séanalee's hand, walked down the stairs and knocked on the counselor's door. When Gale opened the door, I met her gaze and I started crying myself. I don't know why, but I couldn't hold it in. She immediately put her arm around me and said, "Alicia, what's wrong? Are you okay?"

"I'm sorry, Gale. I don't know where the emergency room is, and I don't know how to get there. I am so worried about her and I feel so scared."

She sat me down and explained where I should go, which bus I needed to take and where the urgent care was from the bus stop. She handed me six bus passes and said everything would work out just fine. I felt a little more comfortable after she reassured me I could do it. I still had a lump in my throat, but my heart told my head I could do this. After a couple of hours in urgent care, they called us in and it ended up being that she was allergic to Suprax, the antibiotic the doctor had given her. That was a close call. We got another prescription for amoxicillin and that seemed to work for her.

I felt such relief. Dowser was going to be okay!

I finally got our plane tickets for January 5th until January 17th and I couldn't wait! I called Mount David and told them we were coming home. The excitement I heard in Mammy's voice was great to hear. I couldn't wait to hug everyone, touch them and smell them. But I had a very sick little baby and I knew I had to travel in a couple of days. I was dreading the journey there. It looked like we had eighteen hours there and twenty hours back. There was a seven-hour layover in New York, but at least I would get to go home.

Thank the sweet Lord above.

Whoo Hoo!!!

"Everything that happens to you,

*happens to you for a reason. It happens **for** you.*

Those reasons build strength, times strength,

times strength, which ultimately equals power."

~ Oprah

Chapter 13

Finally, I go back home!

"If you do this Alicia, you may lose the girls altogether. I

would not risk it."

By this time, Jenny also had a baby named Katie who was

two months younger than Séanalee. I could not wait to see

everyone, to hold them and kiss them. It was a very long trip to get

home, but we did it! I was the happiest I had felt in a long, long

time.

This was when Jenny started calling Séanalee *"Flah."*
There is an old Irish song by the Wolfe Tones called *Ooh Ah Up the Ra,* Jenny starting singing *"ooh ah up the flah"* which turned to *"Flah Bug"* and then into *"Buggie"* which is what I call Séanalee to this day.

I had a sense of security and comfort just being with my family. I got to Mount David and Mammy made her usual for me-- a full Irish breakfast! We all sat around the kitchen table and talked about what was going on and how I was going to handle things.

Everyone was there--Mammy, Daddy, Tina, Jenny, Katie, Kim and Amy. We were all united again. 'Tis rare you get a solemn atmosphere in Mammy's kitchen.

We were all eating our breakfast around the table and Jenny started in first. "If I ever see that man again, I will do jail time," she said.

"Not if I get to him first. I would fucken floor him," Daddy exclaimed.

"It's time you tell us what happened, Lysh," Mam said calmly.

I took a deep breath and heard myself shaking as I exhaled. I started from the beginning went through the whole story. I didn't hold back whatsoever. I noticed Mammy was strangely somber and quiet, which is a rarity. Her face was straight with no expression at all. Her eyes told her true emotions, which, I saw, were very sad. I know it must have been such a hard thing for a mother to hear such a story from her child.

For some reason I felt different talking to my family. As I listened to the words come out of my mouth and saw their reactions, I think I started to comprehend the severity of my situation. I just wanted to stay here at home with my babies and never go back there ever, ever again.

Mammy looked at me and asked, "Are you going back, Lysh?"

"I am, Mam. I have to," I replied.

Daddy jumped in and said, "You are home now. You are with your family. You can stay with us and we will mind you. What are they going to do?"

"I know Dad, but I have to go through with this and get divorced from him, if nothing else."

Jenny was beside herself. Her lips were all puckered as if she were sucking on a lemon. She was so angry with the Flatley family and so worried about me, her baby sister.

"It's not right! It's not right, Lysh! What's wrong with these fucking people?" She had the biggest heart and the loudest voice out of all the sisters.

I felt so peaceful at home. My babies were being loved and adored, I had all my sisters, my parents, my cousins and Nana-- everyone who genuinely loved us was around us. It was just an amazing feeling with everyone all together.

We relished in being home. Mammy made all my favourite dinners. Daddy and I would go for a pint together while my girls were at Mount David being watched by the family. I never worried about them the entire time we were home.

As the time grew closer to the trip back to the states, I found myself getting anxious and not wanting to go back. Even though I knew I had to, I just didn't want to go. I was starting to go through scenarios in my head. What if I just didn't get on the plane? What would they do? Would I be looking over my shoulder for the rest of my life? Would I be a criminal? Would the Flatley family come and kidnap the girls?

Even though they were all likely scenarios, I still did not want to go back. I was going back to a battered women's shelter, with no job, having to go to court and worst of all, facing Sean, Anna and Bill. I asked Mammy if I could use the phone and call my lawyer.

I called Katherine and asked her what would happen if I stayed here. She said sternly that there were International Marshalls just for this type of thing. She also said I would be arrested and then might even lose parental rights to the girls. She strongly advised me *NOT* to do it. She said, "If you do this, Alicia, you may lose the girls altogether. I just would not risk it."

As soon as I heard that, I knew I had to go back to the US and take care of my life. Even if I were to be homeless for a while, I would figure it out. I had to. I just had to.

I didn't know it then, but that year would bring me undreamed success.

The day before I had to leave to go back to America, I got a letter in the post from Sean. Even though the restraining order said no contact, he went and wrote me a letter! He said he'd had no choice but to file for divorce. He said he didn't really want one and would like to try and work things out and get back together.

I could not believe what I was reading. The funny thing was I didn't feel any sorrow or sadness that we were getting divorced. I felt free and glad that I was going to get away from his manipulation, judgment, abuse and lies. I showed Mammy the letter and she said to call my lawyer in the states and tell her he'd written to me--and that's exactly what I did. Kathryn said that she would record it for the court and he might be held in contempt.

The next day I asked Mammy to bring me down to Nana's house to visit and say goodbye. I asked if she could drop me off, so I could chat with Nan. I think Mam had her feelings hurt that I asked to go alone, but she seemed to understand. She knew I

needed some one-on-one time with Nana.

Mam called and told her I wanted to visit her alone, so

Nana was prepared to visit with me. When I got to her house she

welcomed me with her warmest embrace.

"Sit down luv. Do you want a little tasheen?" she asked.

"Yes, please Nana, I'd love one," I answered immediately,

almost in desperation.

She handed me a brandy, poured herself one and sat in her

armchair across from me.

"Now, what's on your mind, Alicia? Are you afraid to go

back to America?"

"Oh, Nan, I don't want to go back there. I don't have

anywhere to go. I'm going to stay at the safehouse until the court

date but then I'm not sure what is happening."

"How did ye get to this point, Alicia? What happened? You

know you can tell me," she said softly and genuinely.

So, I told her how things were with Sean and about the

violence and drugs. I didn't hold anything back. I saw her face as I was going through the situations and details of what had happened. She had a soft, dismal look on her face, but she was quiet and allowed me to talk without interruption. I found my voice shaking through some parts of my story, but I didn't cry. I was trying to be strong and show her she did not need to worry about me. But, she knew me inside and out.

She lifted her head, looked at me and said, "Alicia, it makes me happy that you have followed your dreams. You have always had a get-up-and-go about you. You knew you needed more than what Ireland had to offer you and you had the gumption to make that happen. You are a strong woman and now you are a strong Mammy. Don't let anyone stop you from doing what you know is right…because you know it. Its already inside of you, you just have to continue to listen to it. Do you understand what I'm telling you?"

"I think so, Nan."

"What do you think I'm telling you, luv?" she asked, looking at me with one eyebrow raised.

"That I am strong, and I know what is the right thing to do?" I responded.

"Yes, but I also need you to listen and hear that gut feeling. She's your intuition, luv. She will never let you down. Never. Just trust me." Nana said with her serious Danish accent.

"I trust you Nana. I do." I said, submitting to her wisdom.

I had no idea how this conversation and this moment we shared together would impact my life going forward. It was only sheer uncertainty in my future and her voice. Her wisdom would shape and mold my life going forward.

The dreadful day came and we had to leave the Motherland. Both Séanalee and Brennalynn were very sick with coughs and runny noses and we had nineteen hours of travel ahead of us. I had a sense of dread in the pit of my stomach that was firmly planted and not going away. We were getting on a plane in four hours and I did not want to go. I just wanted to stay with my Mam and Dad and all my sisters, all my cousins and my Nana. I was taking my two baby girls into the unknown. I needed to protect them from something and I didn't even know what to

expect.

How was I going to make it by myself?

I packed up the suitcase and put it into the Nissan. I had tea

bags, and Bisto gravy tucked away inside to remind me of home

and bring me some comfort. But saying goodbye to my family this

time was one of the hardest goodbyes ever. Tina, Jenny, Kim and

Amy all held me so tight when we hugged. I didn't want to break

our embrace. If I did I would be all alone and I would have to be

strong for my girls all by myself.

I felt my heart ache like it did after losing Martin Peter and

Mick. I knew if I put in a lot of time thinking about what was

ahead of us I would panic and not have the strength I needed to

have to pull this off. I made a decision to not think about it until I

had to.

Mammy and Daddy gave me some money, about $350.

They really didn't have that much to give but at least I would have

some comfort in not being completely broke and homeless.

The flight back was one of the most toiling things I have

ever faced. Both my babies had a fever and horrible cough. They were both very uncomfortable and cried and screamed a lot on the plane. (That day, I decided that I would never pass judgment on others in a situation like that because nobody knows what you are going through.) People were getting very irritated with me because I had screaming little kids on the plane. I ended up crying myself and breaking down on the trip from New York to Denver. I felt so alone. I felt so scared. My heart ached and I didn't want to leave home.

Why was this happening?

"To get through the hardest journey we need to take only one step at a time, but we must keep on stepping."

~ Chinese proverb

Chapter 14

Facing the World Alone

"Alicia, I have some news.

They performed the test on Sean and it came back

positive. It's cocaine."

Right after I got back to the US, my attorney let me know that because the dissolution of marriage was filed in Adams County she could not work with me on the case because she was located in Boulder County, but she has someone willing to do pro bono in Adams County and he was very good.

I met with Dennis Wanabo and I liked him a lot. He was

such a lovely person. He was more than happy to help me out pro

bono and I was so grateful for him. Dennis also informed me that

Anna and Bill Flatley had retained their own attorney in the case.

They were considered third-party interveners.

I looked at Dennis and asked, "What does that mean

exactly?"

"It means, they are also interested in having some type of

custody of the girls," he replied.

"Are you serious, Dennis? "Why would they do that? I am

not giving anyone my children," I said adamantly.

"Alicia, I feel strongly that this will be a waste of time on

their part. They are paying for two separate attorneys and they

think you don't have an attorney. Everyone received Katherine's

notice about not being able to represent you anymore, but they

have not received my letter of representation yet. Plus, it is only in

extreme circumstances that grandparental rights are enforced. You

have had full custody of your children since they have been born.

You are a very good mother and I plan on making that case," he replied confidently.

"Okay. Dennis, I can't thank you enough for what you are doing for us," I replied with a smile.

He suggested that now would be a good time that we call in the random UA (urine analysis) screening on Sean to make sure he was not doing any drugs. He explained that if Sean really had a problem it would just be a matter of time before he messed up.

So right after my first meeting with Dennis, we called in a UA screening on Sean for the first time. He said that he would call it in and Sean would have twenty-four hours to get tested. This was a Wednesday and they girls were going to go visit the Flatley's on Friday.

Friday morning the phone rang. It was Dennis.

"Alicia, I have some news. They performed the test on Sean and it came back positive. It's cocaine."

I could not believe that he was still on drugs--or maybe I could. Now the courts had proof that he was still on drugs. He was violent and not fit to be around my children. I was in a great position to protect the girls and keep them away from his poison.

Even with this result, I still agreed to let the girls visit their

Grandma and Grandpa every other weekend with the stipulation

that they could not be left alone with Sean. I knew the girls needed

to have a relationship with their grandparents and I was okay with

that, as long as they heeded the guidelines.

I would meet Anna and Bill and let them pick up the girls

for the night. Anna would bring Sean's child support money and

make me sign a piece of paper stating I received this amount on

this date. It was literally her handwriting saying, *I, Alicia Flatley,*

received $185 as child support from Sean Flatley, and a place for

my signature and a date.

After a few weeks of being in the safehouse things started

falling into place. I moved in to an apartment through the

safehouse program. It was quaint, clean, two-bedroom apartment. I

got donations of furniture and coupons to the thrift store from the

shelter. By agreeing to the apartment rules, I would need to attend

the group therapy every Monday across the street at the outreach

center for two years. Séanalee and Brennalynn would attend their counselor at the same time.

I got the girls medical insurance through the state and I was also receiving food stamps for them. I also got a monthly allowance to help with daycare, so all in all things were not that bad. Everything we applied for was coming through all at once. It was great. We moved into our apartment and we loved it!

I got a part-time job as a receptionist in downtown Boulder which was only about a mile's walk from my apartment. It was the same building where Katharine King had her office. I was starting to make friends at work and I felt good about being able to provide for the girls. I only needed assistance with food stamps for three months, and then after that I was able afford to provide for them myself. This was a huge breakthrough and a sense of accomplishment for me. I had full custody of my children, I had a permanent restraining order against Sean and I had control of my life!

We settled nicely into our little apartment. The girls loved it! We would sit and eat dinner together every night. We would have breakfast for dinner most nights as it was Séanalee's favorite supper, and then bath time and reading books together afterward. I could see the contentment and joy in their eyes and nothing could make me happier. I received the majority of things I needed through donations from the safehouse program. Plates, cups, pots and pans, even beds and bedding. I would buy things at the second-hand shop if I really needed them.

We would still meet Anna and Bill every second Friday at a meeting point by my apartment. I did not trust them to keep where we lived from Sean and I didn't want to chance anything. Anna kept asking me to tell her where we lived but I refused.

We would still have to walk or take the bus everywhere in rain, sleet or snow. After a few times walking with my babies in the snow to meet them, Bill said he was going to buy us a car and he did. The next time we went to meet them he had a 1982 silver Subaru hatchback stick shift and handed me the keys. I could not believe it.

Now we had a car! I could drive the girls to daycare and

pick them up. Woo hoo! After Bill gave me the car, Anna kept asking me if she could see the apartment and that she wanted to help me with food and anything else I needed. I finally said yes. I gave her the address and told them they could bring the girls back to the apartment instead of meeting on the street.

That Sunday around 5:00 pm they brought the girls back and brought some groceries and some of Séanalee's stuff from their house. I was still very wary that they would somehow let it slip where we lived and I would get a visit from Sean.

Anna was still giving me money and making me sign a piece of paper saying it was child support. I started saving that money in an old antique jug in the press over the fridge for a rainy day. It started to add up after a few months and I was feeling good about it.

Our lawyers were going back and forth trying to get everything wrapped up and finalized as far as conditions and child support. There was a stipulation in there that I could let Sean see the girls only at his parents' house. He was not allowed to be left alone with them or drive with them and since I had sole custody

Sean would pay $330 per month in child support. I did not know

what I would do with all that money. I was thinking I would buy

brand new bedding for both the girls and maybe a new stroller for

Dowser. I let the safehouse know I was getting child support and

my rent went up because it is 1/3 of my income. I still was able to

have extra cash in the jug at the end of the month.

This lasted maybe two or three months and all of a sudden,

the money stopped coming. I asked Anna if she knew why Sean

had stopped sending the child support and she looked like I had

asked her for blood. She told me Sean had moved to California to

be with his brother Mike and he was looking for a job out there.

I was so relieved to hear he was gone! I know that money

would have helped us a lot, but I didn't care. I wouldn't be looking

over my shoulder or feeling nervous about being found or

followed!

I mentioned to my lawyer Dennis that Sean had and

stopped paying child support and he suggested I call the child

support enforcement unit for Boulder County and open a case with them. I didn't understand fully what they did, but I went ahead and called them. They sent me a pile of paperwork to fill out and send back to them, which I did.

They opened a case for me that had the child support order and kept track of every payment and every non-payment of child support. They would also run his social security number and find him, if he had a job. They would then put in a wage assignment and take the money he was supposed to pay for child support out of his paycheck. So now it was not he-said, she-said. They took care of all of it. This made things so much easier for me.

A few more months passed and I started feeling lonely and missing my family. When Buggie and Dowser would go see their grandparents, I didn't know what to do with myself. I would clean the apartment, but that would only take a couple of hours. I didn't make many friends because I was so enthralled in making my life work and I was adamant I needed to focus on my girls. To be honest, I think I was a still a little timid from what had happened to us.

So I started driving around looking at churches by my

apartment. I found a few of them and wrote down the times of service. Then I went to the thrift store and bought a grown-up bible and a kid's bible. I attended two different churches in one weekend and I liked one more than the other.

The next weekend we got up and had breakfast. I got the girls dressed in pretty dresses and I did their hair in bows and we headed out to try yet a different church. This one said *Seventh Day Adventist* on the outside. We parked and walked in and sat at the back of the church. I did notice there was a separate room in the back for little kids and babies, but I did not want my kids to be in there without me. Service started at 11 am and not kidding you it ended at 3:00 pm. I loved it!!! We were really hungry, but other than that, it was amazing. I loved being there and I felt a sense of purpose. Everything they said made sense to me.

There were some major differences from my strict Roman Catholic upbringing, like perhaps their most obvious practice which differentiates them from most other Christian churches-- they observe Saturday as their weekly Sabbath. You cannot have any outside influences during Sabbath, which means no TV, radio, or telephone. Just read the Bible and be with loved ones. They also read the book of Revelations, which we were forbidden to read in our church at home. I started feeling wronged by my church at home and liking my new church here in America.

This carried on for a few months. I would read the Bible to the girls at night instead of nursery rhymes. We would not do anything but worship God on the Sabbath day. I started doubting Catholicism in general and I felt it was such a contradiction to the Bible itself.

Then one weekend my phone rang and it was Tina. She had moved to NY with Gerard after they were married. It was great talking to her. She was about five or six months pregnant and with twins! As the conversation progressed, she mentioned that she would be sending Séanalee and Brennalynn some Easter eggs for Easter and I said, "No TT, we don't celebrate Easter anymore. I don't want you sending the girls Easter eggs or Christmas presents."

There was silence on the other end of the phone for about

ten seconds and then I literally heard her screaming…

"What the fuck are you doing, Alicia? It sounds to me like you are part of a fecken cult! If you are, I am on the next plane out there, do you hear me? I can, and I will, send my godchild and my niece Easter eggs, and you WILL give it to them!"

"God almighty, Tina, will you calm down?" I said.

"Alicia, that's it! I'm coming to Colorado to see you. I am worried about you, worried sick!" she sternly said to me.

"Really TT? You will?"

I was so excited that I would see my big sister after all these months of being alone.

Suddenly, I felt maybe I didn't need church that much after all. TT was coming! TT was coming! Now I had something to look forward to--my sister was coming to see us! It was almost like a light switch that flipped, or my Crone Voice whispered it to me maybe family is my church.

By the time Tina got her ticket to come out to see me, she

was seven months pregnant with the twins. It was snowing and cold. I had the entire house cleaned and I had food in the fridge and my heart was bursting waiting for her. I had Séanalee and Brennalynn dressed beautifully and I plaited Séanalee's hair and put a bow on it. Brennalynn's was too short so I combed it to the side and had a pretty clip in it. We drove to the airport and parked the car and walked in to wait for her to come through the doors. I was working on getting the girls excited to see Aunty TT.

"Séanalee, Aunty TT is coming. Can you see her? Where is Aunty TT? Brennalynn can you see her?" I said to them. Both of them were looking at everyone's faces to see if it was their Aunty. Then I saw her. There she was, all pregnant and beautiful! I grabbed both the girls' arms and almost dragged them to run over and see my sister. Finally, we had our arms around each other, hugging as tight as can be. We looked at each other and we were both crying like babies with happy tears.

Tina looked at the girls and said, "Oh my God, Séanalee. My Godchild, you are so pretty. Dowser, you are walking like a big girl!"

"Yep, she is a big girl," Séanalee said, being the big sister she was at almost four years old! Tina went to pick up Brennalynn.

I said, "Janey Mackers, Tina, will you put her down? You can't be lifting up Dowser with two babies in your tummy."

"Yerra, I am all right, Lysh. I'll know if it gets too much," she replied.

We were all on cloud nine. We walked out to the car, loaded Tina's bags and headed on our way to our little apartment in Boulder. After we got home, I made some tea and biscuits and we just sat together catching up. Poor ol' Tina looked exhausted. Her eyes were hanging out of her head. I put the girls down to bed for the night and got my PJ's on. When I came out to the sitting room, TT had dozed off. I cleaned up the kitchen and woke her up to go to bed.

She slept in my bed with me, so we ended up talking until about midnight. I had to get up for work the next day and Tina wanted to be home with the girls. I really did not want to go to work but I had to.

I raced home after I was finished and I walked in the door of the apartment. Tina had a full dinner ready. The entire table was set and she had placed wildflowers that she and the girls picked for me at the park earlier. That was one of the warmest memories I have of being at the apartment. Tina made it feel like home. We had the most wonderful time together for the entire trip.

We had quality time together, all of us. The girls loved their aunt's attention and love. Tina even came with me to my lawyer's office and met Dennis. She insisted we buy him some Irish whiskey and get him good Irish crystal whiskey glasses, so she did. Boy, he loved it. On the last day Tina was with me, we decided to make a video sitting on the couch and reflect on her trip here and what we did.

We were making it for Ireland, so they could see us together. I swear, we laughed so much I thought she might go into labor and give birth to the twins right then and there. We still have that tape today--in VHS mind you--and it is just as funny as it was that night. So that's what I needed after all--a good dose of family.

After Tina went back to New York, I felt more secure and self-assured in some way. I started being more open with people at work and actually started making friends. I felt my mojo was coming back and I was not timid and scared, which is what I had been feeling for a few years. I just felt good.

That confidence showed at work and before you know it, in my job as a receptionist, I was joking with and making friends with the other receptionists. There was Shannon, Robin, Carly, Sara and me. All of the receptionists were young and they used to go out together after work around Boulder. I never did, because I was always anxious to go home to the girls. We all worked part-time. There was the morning shift and the afternoon shift. I started to work more with Sara, who was a beautiful person. You know you can tell when someone is kind and genuine?

I didn't advertise my living situation. I kind of kept it close and personal, but everyone knew I was a single mother. There is one memory that has stayed with me throughout the years. I was at work and I got a call from Jumping Gyminee Daycare. They said I needed to go and pick up Séanalee, that she had a temperature of 103. I had just started my shift, and I panicked that I had to go and be with my daughter. I couldn't find Shannon, our supervisor, but I couldn't wait.

When I saw Sara I told her I got a call and I had to go get my daughter right away. My voice immediately started quivering. I was trying to ask her to let Shannon know I had to leave. A tear rolled down my cheek. The hurt I felt was so real in my heart. I just needed to go get my daughter.

Sara looked at me and said, "You go get your baby and don't worry about anything. I will cover your shift and I'll let Shannon know what's going on."

I thanked Sara and ran out to my car with tears in my eyes. I rushed over to the Jumping Gyminee, which was clear across at the other end of Boulder and then I walked in to get her.

There was my little Buggie with rosy cheeks, lying down sucking her thumb. I picked her up and hugged her. The heat was radiating from her and I started crying harder. I got Brennalynn and put them in their car seats to take them home.

Once we got home, I called the doctor's office and told them Buggie was sick with a fever. They said to give her a warm bath, baby Tylenol and lots of fluids and if her fever was still there in the morning I would have to bring her into the office.

So I did just that. I put some clean PJ's on her and made her favorite supper, a boiled egg in a cup with toast and tea. She had no appetite at all. My heart ached seeing her so ill. I fed Brennalynn and put on Séanalee's favorite movie, *The Land Before Time*, in my room in the hopes that Séanalee would fall asleep. We all laid down on my bed and I was cuddling with them watching the movie.

Séanalee looked so sick. She looked at me with her sad eyes and said, "Mommy, my three horn hurts." I giggled and kissed her forehead. I realized she was calling her forehead her three horn, just like Luna in the movie *The Land Before Time*.

About halfway through watching it, I heard a knock on the

door. My heart was in my mouth. Nobody knew where I lived except the Flatley's. I didn't have any way of knowing who it was until I actually opened the door because there was no peephole on it.

Slowly, I got up from bed so as not to wake up Séanalee. Brennalynn was just happy lying down with her hands behind her head like Lady Muck. I closed the bedroom door, grabbed the phone and went to the front door, opening it with my fingers and ready to dial 911. Standing just outside my door was Sara from work with two shopping bags in her hands.

"Hi, Alicia. I really hope you are not upset with me. I looked in the files at work to get your address," she said sincerely.

"Oh, my goodness, Sara, come in. What's going on? Is everything okay?" I asked her.

"Yes, everything is fine. I just wanted to bring you some supplies for your little girl who's sick. I couldn't stop thinking of you after you left, and I knew you were very worried. I picked up some chicken noodle soup, ginger ale, children's Tylenol, crackers and popsicles for her, and if you need anything else I can run out and get it for you."

"Wow, Sara! I cannot believe your kindness. I don't know what to say," I replied.

"You can say... would you like a cup of tea, Sara?" she said.

And there was the beginning of a new friendship--you know, the kind of friendships that are keepers, the ones you take for granted just by having them.

Yep that was Sara Maranowicz. I told Sara about my journey in life so far and how we got there, and her empathy and genuine compassion was just awe-inspiring to me. It's still something I strive for on a daily basis.

Sara and I became solid friends. She insisted we come to her house for Thanksgiving and meet her family and we did. We were welcomed year after year with open arms and great home-cooked food. Bob and Kay, Sara's parents, were such wonderful people. Now I understood where Sara got her demeanor. Her sister Amy had it, too. This was the definition of a loving, kind family.

"Kindness is a currency well beyond riches."

~ Alicia McMahon

Chapter 15

Chasing that American Dream

"I certainly will not! My Mother raised me better than

that! I'm not going into yer room, but ye can bring me

out a beer if ye want."

I was still working at Broadway Suites as a receptionist for

about twenty-eight hours per week. I was able to take up some

extra work for people in the building, help with writing transcripts

for the attorneys, filling in for extra cash and taking on special

projects as needed.

I had a lot of new friends and acquaintances. One of the tenants in the building was Carrie Van Heyst, Suite 302. I would see Carrie every day because her office was right beside the reception desk. We would chat all the time and I found her to be very warm and intelligent. We went to lunch a few times and became fast friends. Carrie's company is called The Van Heyst Group.

One day she had asked me if I was interested in some extra work and of course I said yes. She needed help on one of her events that was being held in Aspen, which is about five hours from Boulder. I was so excited. It was a Fortune 500 conference they were hosting and she needed someone to be the War Room Manager...ME! I had to take a day off work from Broadway Suites, but it was worth it for the extra cash. Carrie explained to me what the job of War Room Manager would entail and then she told me what she would pay me for the three days' work...one-thousand dollars! I thought I'd hit the lottery, really.

That was more money that I made in two months of work at Broadway Suites. I called Anna and asked if Séanalee and

Brennalynn could stay with them while I went to Aspen from Thursday to Sunday and of course they said yes.

I wrote down the directions from Boulder and headed up to the Ritz Carlton Hotel in Aspen. It took about six hours to drive through the mountains. I left after work on Wednesday because I got off at 2:00 pm, and I arrived around 8:15 pm at the hotel.

This was my first time in a really nice hotel and I could not believe it. It was spectacular. There were marble floors you could see your face in. There was a massive arrangement of exotic flowers in the center of the lobby. They also had a huge fireplace with real leather sitting chairs and a chandelier that looked like it should have been in a caste!

I checked into my room and went down to the conference area. Now I understood why they called it a *War Room*. There were already people there from New York from the Fortune magazine conference division and it was nuts.

I knew I had to do whatever it took to manage this room. I looked at the dossier and was blown away. Colin Powell, Bill

Clinton, Madeleine Albright, Kenneth Lay and other major lead Wall Street players were attending. Even a young upstart named Jeff Bezos was on the attendance sheet.

Carrie was on her laptop at the end of the huge conference table. She got up when I walked into the room and introduced me to everyone. It was 9:00 pm and I stayed until well after midnight making sure the gift bags for the participants were collated and marked. I made sure there were enough office supplies and refreshments set up for the next day. I updated the agenda and checked security for Colin Powell's and Bill Clinton' s arrival the next day. I worked hard, and I tried to apply myself as much as possible.

When I returned to my room at night, my feet would be so sore because the dress shoes I was wearing were too small for me. I had picked them up at a secondhand shop before I left.

The next morning, I had to be up at 5:30 am and set up registration with the folks from New York and finish making the lanyards before 7:00 am. It was a long, long day and I was exhausted! Carrie was more involved with the keynote speakers and content, so I didn't see her much during the first day because everyone was so busy.

I could not believe who was attending this conference. This was a big deal. Ben Affleck was scheduled to speak on his greenlight project so there were some paparazzi outside the hotel, but we got word that he checked into rehab the night before. I'm glad he got help but he made my job a lot harder. Hollywood types!

The next morning was another 5:30 am start for me and we were wrapped up by 6:00 pm. Carrie told me that everyone from Fortune 500 conference division and the Van Heyst Group usually got together and did something fun once the conference was over. I was to be in the lobby of the hotel at 7:00 am wearing warm clothes.

This was so exciting. We all met in the lobby and we were told to get into the Stretch SUV's waiting outside for all of us. The limos convoyed through the small streets of Aspen and pulled up outside a bar. We all got out and there was a row of tequila shots for all of us. We were there about five minutes and then were instructed to go back into the SUV's. We drove for about ten minutes outside the town and we pulled into a big ranch--you know, with the big arch at the entrance of the property. We got out of the cars again and we were greeted by four legitimate cowboys on horses. They informed us that we were all going to ride up the mountain on a horse and there would be food and entertainment waiting for us at the top.

We were all provided with our own horses and we had to follow our guide.

The scenery was just spectacular. I'd never actually soaked in Colorado like this before. It was so much fun. I laughed practically the entire way up there. Patty was Carrie's sister and she got the small *rogue horse* that just would not cooperate.

It was hilarious. I can still see the picture in my head of Patty's legs going up in the air a few times as the small rogue horse took off. Patty kept saying, "What is wrong with this horse? He is broken. I want a different one."

She would look at me and I couldn't hold my laughter in.

That horse was relentless--he just kept disobeying her and not following the group. I would say at least six times she was taken off the trail. I was laughing so hard my stomach hurt and I was crying with laughter. I am giggling right now writing this. It was priceless.

By the time we reached the top of the mountain, it was just starting to get dark. At the top there was a big campfire, picnic tables, a couple of chefs with barbecues, a bartender and musicians with banjos and guitars.

We had a blast. We ate, drank, sang and danced. There were three 4x4 vehicles to take us all back down the mountain. We had to hold on to the bars in the back of the excursion vehicles and it was open like on a truck bed. That was a bumpy ride back down the mountain.

The next morning, we were told to meet again in the lobby for our last surprise, which was white water rafting! This was the most fun I have ever had in twenty-four hours.

That weekend opened up something special for me--

opportunity and friendship with Carrie and the Van Heyst Group. Carrie asked me to do another event in Palo Alto, California with her and I was ecstatic about it. Of course, I would.

I was able to take a couple of days off from Broadway Suites as Sara covered my shifts for me. Once again, Anna and Bill were excited about watching the girls. It was at this time that I realized I might be able to have a career with this.

I continued to work for The Van Heyst Group on and off, whenever Carrie asked me to. I was so happy and grateful to be a part of it, I would have done anything to help out.

The Van Heyst Group also had a partnership with Fortune 500 Conference Division and they had a conference in Boston at the Four Seasons Hotel. This happened to be the same time as the kick off to the Rolling Stones Comeback Tour in 1998. The conference was being held on the 5th floor of the hotel and the Rolling Stones had the 5th floor wing. You needed a security pass to access the 5th floor elevator.

I was so exhausted organizing everything in the office. I would be up at 5:30 am and closing down the War Room at about

9 or 10:00 pm.

The first day of set up was a long one. We took a break for dinner and I still had some gift bags to finish before morning. I went back to the War Room and finished up around 11:15 pm. I went up to my room, showered, got into my Winnie the Pooh PJ's and flopped onto the bed. My hair was wet and I didn't care. I was cooked.

After about fifteen minutes, I heard loud music being played in the room next door. Loud music, as in with amplifiers and big bass shaking the floor. I realized I was the last room on the floor before the wing that must be the band. I tried to ignore it, but it was loud. I got up, went out to the hall and turned the corner and there was a bodyguard standing outside these double doors. He spotted me as soon as I turned the corner and was staring at me as I walked closer to him. He looked like the fella from the Green Mile standing there with his arms crossed.

I walked up to him and said, "How's it goin? I am in the room next door. Listen--is there any chance you could ask them to turn off the amplifiers or at least turn them down? I have to be up

in five hours and it's really loud in my room."

He looked at me from my feet all the way up to my wet

head and said, "I'm not asking them to do that, but you can."

"Grand, so," I said, just then realizing I was still in my

Winnie the Pooh PJs' and had wet hair. I knocked on the door and

they obviously didn't hear it, so the bodyguard banged loudly on

the door to back me up. The music stopped and I heard someone

walking towards the door. The door opened, and it was Ronnie

Woods. You should have seen his face. I think once he saw the

bodyguard still there, he was relieved.

He looked at me and asked me, "Can I help you?"

Just then, Keith Richards stuck his head around the corner

to see what was going on and then walked up behind him.

I looked at them and said, "Howr'a Lads? I'm in the room

next door. Is there any chance ye could turn down the music a bit?

I have to be up in a few hours."

"Well, well, well, do we have a wee Irish lass amongst us?"

Keith Richards asked.

"You do," I replied.

Ronnie stepped back and said, "Come in. Come in and grab a beer."

"I certainly will not! My Mother raised me better than that. I'm not going into yer room," I said with a smile on my face. "But ye can bring me out a beer if ye want," I said half-jokingly.

Sure enough, Ronnie grabbed three beers and we sat in the foyer on the floor between our rooms and drank fecken Miller Light! Of all beers they could be drinking, fecken Miller Light.

They were super nice people. Ronnie was telling me about the renovations he and his wife were doing in his house and they couldn't use the kitchen for weeks. He said he was glad to be on tour because his wife was driving him mad. As for Keith, he laughed a lot. I truly couldn't make out a complete sentence from him, but I could make out enough. I did notice that the lines in Keith's face are probably the deepest facial lines I have ever seen.

They offered me VIP tickets to go backstage with them the next night, but I explained I couldn't go because I was working.

At one-point Mick Jagger and their tour manager got off the elevator and strutted in. He looked at me like I was a crazy woman or groupie. Ronnie said I was from Ireland and had the room next door. It seemed like Mick had no time for that jibber jabber. I stood up and thanked them for my beer and wished them all the best.

The next morning one of their bodyguards came into the War Room where I was working and asked for me. He had an 8x10 photo of Keith Richards with *"To one cool Irish Lass, love Keith,"* written on it. I put it up on my desk above the picture of Séanalee and Brennalynn with a note saying *Alicia's boyfriend* and an arrow pointing to the picture. Gosh, when I think about that right now, it just puts a smile on my face.

I started working more and more for the Van Heyst Group and eventually Carrie asked me to come on board as a full-time employee. They had just landed a big contract with Microsoft for Bill Gates' Personal CEO Summit. I was now Executive Relations Manager and I had an office on the fourth floor of Broadway

Suites. I was no longer the part-time receptionist downstairs where I started. This was such a huge opportunity for me. Carrie and I became a lot closer. She brought me to a different level of professionalism.

I was exposed to some amazing people during my time working on Bill Gates' CEO Summits. Warren Buffet, who called me the Irish lass, Colin Powell, Martha Stewart, Michael Eisner, Steve Jobs and Bill Clinton were all in attendance.

I became more familiar with the participants and speakers. By the second year I said to myself, *Wow! Here I am, Alicia McMahon, who was literally homeless not too long ago with two babies, one nappy bag and $13 to my name, from a little village in Ireland--and now standing next to Warren Buffet and he actually knows my name!*

It was the 1998 Conference and Ted Turner had just donated $1 Billion to United Nation Agencies. He was one of the keynote speakers.

I had to greet Ted and Jane Fonda and escort them to the stage, let them know the process of getting mic'd up and introduce them to the backstage IT team, etc. I was star struck, even more so with Jane Fonda, I think. I was just finishing up the quick orientation with them and I told them if there was anything they needed, just let me know.

Right after I said that, Ted Turner looked right at me and asked, "What's your accent, are you British?"

"No, no, Mr. Turner. I am Irish, and I won't hold it against you that you thought I was British," I said jokingly with a smile on my face and my eyebrows raised.

"What did she say?" He asked Jane.

"She said she is Irish and she will forgive you for asking if she was British," Jane yelled back at him.

He looked directly at me with his piercing blue eyes and big, bushy white eyebrows and right at that second, I thought I was in deep trouble. Then he smiled and said, "I like your spunk! And you can call me Ted. My father was Mr. Turner."

"Thanks very much, Ted," I graciously replied, delighted

that I hadn't overstepped my boundaries.

"Now, is there anything else ye need before I go back to the registration?" I asked.

"Well, I would love a cup of tea," Ted said, looking at Jane.

"You know that would be lovely. Would you join us, Alicia?" Jane asked.

"I would absolutely love to join you, but I think I'm needed out front at the moment," I replied.

"They can wait! We would like to have spot of tea and a crumpet with my Irish friend," Ted said in an English accent.

"All right, so, if anything I need to explain the difference between an Irish accent and an English accent to you," I replied.

We found a table and I had the hotel bring us some tea and pastries. We sat and talked. I didn't realize Ted Turner was so hard of hearing. Everything I said to them, Jane had to repeat loudly in his ear. I found Jane to be so elegant and beautiful--the quintessential classy movie star.

I didn't ask about his speech, his $1 billion donations or

anything business-related. I asked about his family and how they met. It was a real nice conversation. After about ten minutes, David from the registration desk came over, apologized for interrupting and said that Martha Stewart had a question for me about security. I told David I would be right there.

I thanked both Jane and Ted for the tea and asked if they and any advice for me trying to make my life in the U.S. I can't remember everything they said, but I will never forget Jane telling me, "Your life is your canvas and you are the only one who can paint that picture."

The next day we had to transport the participants to Bill Gates' house for dinner and then on back to the hotel. I checked everyone on the bus to go to the Gates' residence except for Michael Eisner, who was the CEO of Disney at the time—and he was giving a speech. We had Gates security and secret service and local law enforcement waiting for my thumbs up that the bus had left the hotel. I was getting nervous. Where was Michael Eisner?

I was just about to send the bus on its way when Michael

ran over to me. He was obviously out of breath. "Alicia, I have a huge favor to ask of you," he said, panting trying to catch his breath.

"Of course, what do you need, Mr. Eisner?" I replied immediately.

"I am speaking in forty-five minutes and I cannot find my glasses. I can't read my speaking points without them. Could I ask you to go up to my room and search for them, please?"

"Of course!" I said. "Are you sure they are in your room?"

"Yes. I had them this afternoon in the room."

He handed me his room key and said, "I apologize in advance for the state of the room. It's a bit of a mess."

"Don't worry about it at all," I replied as I led him onto the bus. I radioed security and cleared the bus to travel to the Gates' residence.

Then I went straight up to the third floor and entered his room. Gosh, he wasn't kidding about the room--it looked ransacked. The misfortune. He must have been looking for the glasses in a frenzy. I checked all around the bathroom, under the chairs, under the bed and pillows but nothing was there. I rummaged through his suitcase and closet.

It felt pretty weird being inside the CEO of Disney's room riffling through his personal belongings. I was just about to give up when I pulled out the couch cushions and there they were! I ran downstairs and called for one of the black town cars over my radio. I delivered them to Michael just in time for his speech. I could see he was so appreciative and grateful.

All was good, crisis averted. Phew!

Later that evening after the conference, one of the hotel staff called out my name. They were standing with Mr. Eisner. I walked over to them and he shook my hand and put his other hand on top of our hand shake and said, "I really appreciate how you went above and beyond to save my keister today, Alicia. Thank you!"

I received a bouquet of flowers in my room the next day with a lovely note from him.

"Thank you for getting me out of a pickle yesterday!

Warmest Regards, Michael E."

When I look at all of these influential beings, business tycoons and world leaders, I realize they are really not that different from any one of us. Whether it's complaining about renovations at your house and arguing with your spouse, being hard of hearing or losing your reading glasses, we all put our pants on one leg at a time.

"Have manners and respect. Keep your philosophy

simple.

Be kind."

~ Alicia McMahon

The Conclusion

Derived from the Greek word Triskeles meaning three legs, the **Triskele** or Triple Spiral is a complex ancient Celtic symbol. Often referred to by many as a **Triskelion**, its earliest creation dates back to the Neolithic era, as it can be seen at the entrance of Newgrange, Ireland.

The Triskele is the symbol for the stages in a woman's life and it's all coming from one center intertwined by the never-ending circle of life. This is a connection that carries from one generation to the next. I feel genuinely drawn to this symbol and it in its beauty as it shows the stages in a woman's life from Maiden to Mother to Crone. With this journey comes an inherent wisdom

that you cannot assume or will for yourself. It comes with going

through the stages of exploration, mistakes, eagerness, failures and

achievements. But that center holds guidance and Insight that we

all have. We just need to listen and trust it. I have deemed mine my

Crone Voice which I identify as my Nana Murphy. I hope that I

will be that center for my girls one day.

Life is so unpredictable. No matter what type of situation

we find ourselves in during our journey. Have you ever heard

anyone say, *I shouldn't have listened to my inside voice*? Yep, me

neither.

I think back to my last night with Nana Murphy when I

tucked her in for the evening by the fire. I closed the front door

behind me and stepped out into the night. I looked up at the dark

Irish sky and felt the bitter cold breeze coming from the Shannon

Estuary on my face, the sound of roaring tree tops coming from

Foynes woods.

Now the memory of that feeling always makes me smile. I started to cross the road to Mutt's house, but filling my empty glass wasn't what I was thinking about anymore. I was thinking about what Nana said. I might never know what that beautiful old woman actually meant, but in my heart and soul I'm sure I will figure it out.

I will always be **The Maiden**. Growing up in Foynes and Shanagolden, I got into shenanigans, and then I set out on my own journey. I wouldn't trade my time in England, France or going to the USA for anything!
Even though the world might not see me as that young, foolish, brave full of energy girl anymore, she is still in my heart and part of me.

But times change, people change. I changed. Then I became *The Mother.* We don't get to pick what life has in store for us, but we have an inherent drive to protect our young and set an example for behavior and strength.

I will always be Séanalee and Brennalynn's Mammy. I am their **Mother** even after I'm long gone. They have their own lives to navigate and experience and I must allow them to live their lives. Lives I can't wait to see play out! The three of us had a challenging but wonderful life together with many ups and downs. Sadness and happiness. Failures and triumphs. But it was our lives to live.

My two beautiful Maidens have made me so proud, my heart swells with love and respect for both of them. I have such an appreciation for who they are as individuals and now blossoming as adults. They have traveled this journey with me every step of the way, and now they are well on their way to creating their own lives, their own journeys and experiencing their own chapters.

I think I get it now… I need to allow them to develop their own intuition and trust in their own voice. That is something I cannot control, but I can help them like Nana helped me.

After the Maiden, after the Mother, I can't wait for my next journey into the ultimate honour of hopefully being **The Crone.**

How lucky am I?

How grateful am I?

How proud am I?

Now, begs the question…

Who am I?

After some practice and true self-reflection, you will not only recognize your voice, but you will learn to trust it. I'm sure basing your actions on something that can be as unquantifiable as reflection might make you nervous. The beauty of reflection is that it will not steer you wrong. It will actually give you the most truthful and clear guidance you will ever have.

~ Alicia McMahon

Thank you for reading my story!

CPSIA information can be obtained
at www.ICGtesting.com
Printed in the USA
LVHW091750280319
612190LV00004B/837/P

9 781642 544688